# APOLLO

ROBIN KERROD

MALLARD
PRESS

This book was devised and produced by
Multimedia Books Limited

**Editor: Linda Osband**
**Design: John Strange**
**Production: Zivia Desai**

First published in the United States of America in
1989 by Mallard Press.

Mallard Press and its accompanying design and
logo are trademarks of BDD Promotional Book
Company, Inc.

ISBN 0-792-45038-8

Typeset by BWS Typesetters, London
Origination by Imago Publishing Limited
Printed in Italy by Imago Publishing Limited

# Contents

# 'Before This Decade Is Out'

THE GREATEST ADVENTURE OF ALL time began on 25 May 1961. On that day John Fitzgerald Kennedy, 35th President of the United States, delivered before a joint session of Congress an impassioned plea for the US to spare no effort to achieve pre-eminence in space. He had a specific goal in mind.

Even while campaigning for the Presidency the previous year, Kennedy had enthused about the rapidly accelerating thrust into space, which was developing into a race between the United States and Russia. Said Kennedy then: 'We cannot run second in this vital race. To insure peace and freedom, we must be first. This is the new age of exploration. Space is our great new frontier.'

But as Kennedy took office in January 1961, at 43 the youngest man ever to become President, the United States was running a poor second in a two-horse race. Came April, and Russia lofted the first human being into space, Yuri Gagarin. A few days later, CIA-backed Cuban rebels were routed as they tried to oust communist President Fidel Castro at the Bay of Pigs.

These events combined to reduce American morale to a low ebb. This did not fit in with the Kennedy vision of a vigorous New World. American pride and self-esteem had to be restored. And that is what prompted him to make his historic speech before Congress on 25 May.

'Space is open to us now,' said Kennedy, 'and our eagerness to share its meaning is not governed by the efforts of others. We go into space because whatever man must undertake, free men must fully share.

'I believe that this nation should commit itself to achieving the goal, before this decade is out, of landing a man on the Moon and returning him safely to Earth.

'No single space project in this period will be more impressive to mankind, or more important for the long-range exploration of space; and none will be so difficult or expensive to accomplish. It will not be one man going to the Moon, it will be an entire nation.'

The President carried Congress and the 'entire nation' with him, and the Apollo Moon-landing program was underway. In the following chapters we trace the story of Apollo from that May day in Washington to the lava plains of the Moon's Sea of Tranquillity, where Apollo 11 first made lunar landfall before the decade was out.

Tragically, President John F. Kennedy did not live to see his dream become reality. On 22 November 1963 he was cut down by an assassin's bullet in Dallas, Texas. Afterwards, Moon- rocket designer Wernher von Braun said of the President: 'He made the country feel young again.' This was as fine an epitaph as any for the man whose youthful vigor and vision launched a fleet of spaceships to another world on the greatest adventure of all time.

◀ First-man-on-the-Moon Neil Armstrong is reflected in the gold-tinted vizor of second-man-in-the-Moon Edwin Aldrin in this most famous photograph taken at Tranquillity Base on 20 July 1969. Also reflected is the Apollo 11 lunar module *Eagle*.

▶ Speaking before Congress on 25 May 1961, President Kennedy exhorts the nation to go for the Moon.

# Making Haste Slowly

# ONE

PRESIDENT KENNEDY'S CHALLENGE thrown at the American people in May 1961 – land a man on the Moon and do it by the end of the decade – seemed to most people at the time an impossible target. As yet no American had even been launched into orbit a few hundred kilometers around the Earth. So what prospect was there of one flying hundreds of thousands of kilometers to the Moon?

However, the three-year-old NASA (National Aeronautics and Space Administration) thought otherwise. It had already embarked on the Mercury project to get an American into orbit. And indeed it had already earmarked lunar exploration as a goal for the not-too-distant future. It had even selected a name for the project to follow Mercury – Project Apollo.

After Kennedy's speech, Apollo became specifically a Moon-landing program. But it soon became clear that a jump from Mercury directly to Apollo would be too great, so an intermediate program, Gemini, was conceived and announced in December 1961.

By this time two Americans had made suborbital flights, but only a chimpanzee had made it into orbit. Not until February 1962 did American manned spaceflight become a reality when John Glenn soared into orbit in a Mercury capsule. America was on its way to the Moon – but, oh, so slowly.

Just three more US manned flights took place over the next four years. Only when the Gemini program lifted off in March 1965 did the impetus into orbit start to build up. As the program progressed Americans learned the art of spacewalking; performed rendezvous and docking maneuvers with consummate ease; and generally began to get the feel of space. By the time Gemini ended in 1966, Kennedy's goal seemed no longer impossible but quite achievable.

▶ Gemini 4 astronaut Edward White makes the first American spacewalk on 3 June 1965. He remains outside his spacecraft for 20 minutes. The view, he said, is 'worth a million dollars'. The apparatus he is holding is a gas-gun for maneuvering.

◀ David Scott (left) and Neil Armstrong wait patiently in their Gemini 8 capsule after splashdown on 16 March 1966 as the flotation collar is placed in position. Earlier they had performed, albeit briefly, the first in-orbit docking.

◀ Mercury astronaut Alan Shepard is winched out of his capsule *Freedom 7* and up to the recovery helicopter after a 15-minute lob into space and back. The date is 5 May 1961.

### The 'Original Seven'

NASA announced the establishment of a national manned space flight project on 7 October 1958, just six days after its formation. The following month the project became known as Mercury. In April 1959 the names of the first seven astronauts were announced: Scott Carpenter, Gordon Cooper, John Glenn, Virgil Grissom, Walter Schirra, Alan Shepard and Donald Slayton. They were all military personnel, most of them highly experienced test and fighter pilots with the 'Right Stuff', the crème de la crème of the flying corps. When they went into space, it would be as test pilots, flying a cramped 'tin can' of a capsule little bigger than a telephone booth to face unknown hazards in orbit at speeds of 28,000 km/h (17,500 mph).

It was perhaps inevitable that Russia would get there first. It had beaten the US in launching its first Sputnik (4 October 1957) nearly four months before the US launched its first satellite, Explorer 1 (31 January 1958). And on 12 April 1961 Russia launched the first man into orbit, Yuri Gagarin. Pioneering cosmonaut Gagarin made one orbit of the Earth in his capsule Vostok 1. But less than a month later on 5 May, the US salvaged a vestige of pride by launching Alan Shepard in a Mercury capsule (named *Freedom 7*) on a 15-minute suborbital flight. But Russian premier Nikita Khrushchev contemptuously called it 'a flea jump'.

To President Kennedy, Gagarin's flight proved the last straw, and that is why in May he urged Congress and the American people to reach for the Moon.

In July Virgil Grissom made a second suborbital flight in Mercury capsule *Liberty Bell 7*, which went according to the book until right at the end. Minutes after splashing down, the capsule sank, fortunately not before Grissom was whisked to safety. (All Mercury capsule names were followed by the number 7, after the 'Original Seven' astronauts.)

### The Mercury flights – one by one

The stated objectives of Project Mercury appear modest to us now, but at the time seemed formidable. They were: (1) to place a manned spacecraft in orbit around the Earth. (2) To investigate man's ability to function in space. (3) To recover the man and the spacecraft safely.

These basic objectives were first met when John Glenn made a successful three-orbit flight on 20 February 1962. He became the third man to orbit the Earth, after cosmonauts Yuri Gagarin (12 April 1961, 1 orbit) and Gherman Titov (6 August 1961, 17 orbits). In his capsule *Friendship 7*, he was blasted off the launch pad by an Atlas rocket and spent nearly five hours in space before splashing down at sea, the way all American astronauts would return to Earth until the shuttle era.

The flight was not without its problems. He reported it was a little bumpy at times, but loved the view! The attitude control system played up and he had to take over manual control. Telemetry told ground control that there would be serious problems with the heat shield. But, although Glenn reported that during re-entry there was 'a real fireball outside', the heat shield held.

Predictably, Glenn was fêted on his return. In New York City alone four million people attended a ticker-tape parade in his honor. At a welcoming ceremony at the White House President Kennedy congratulated the space hero but warned: 'We have a long way to go in this space race. But this is the new ocean, and I believe the United States must sail on it and be in a position second to none.'

As if to prove Glenn's flight was no fluke, Scott Carpenter put in a repeat three-orbit mission in *Aurora 7* on 24 May. Walter Schirra's flight, in *Sigma 7* on 3 October, was twice as long. And Project Mercury ended with a 22-orbit, 34-hour flight by Gordon Cooper in *Faith 7* on 15/16 May 1963.

So far, so good. In isolation, the US space effort would seem to have been progressing well. But compared with the accelerating Russian space effort, which had put five men and one woman into orbit for a total of over two weeks, Mercury was an also-ran.

▶ Gordon Cooper in *Faith 7* blasts off the launch pad at Cape Canaveral on 15 May 1963 on the final flight in Project Mercury. He returns next day after completing a record, for the Americans, 22 orbits of the Earth.

▼ Squeezing into the cramped interior of the Mercury capsule *Friendship 7* on 20 February 1962 is John Glenn, shortly to become the first American to go into orbit.

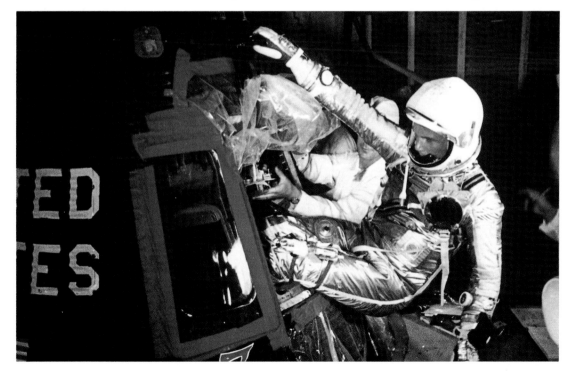

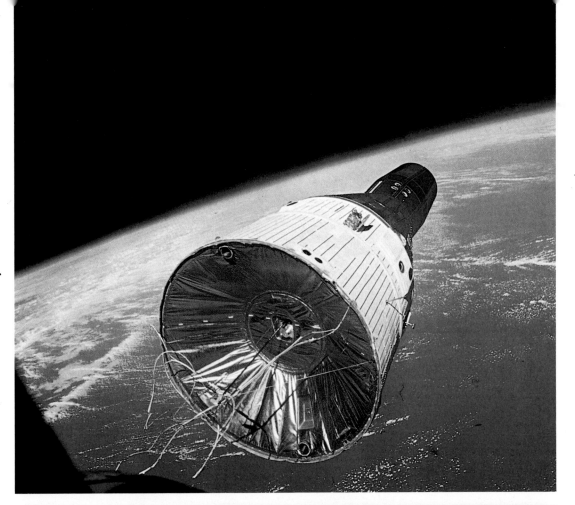

◀ Gemini astronauts pioneer the art of orbital photography, snapping stunning scenes all over the globe. The Gemini 9 astronauts take this spectacular shot of India and at bottom right Sri Lanka (Ceylon).

### The Gemini program – two by two

But things are not always what they seem. Behind the scenes work was progressing well on Gemini, the follow-up program that would lay firm foundations for Apollo. In contrast to Mercury, the Gemini capsule carried a crew of two (hence the name Gemini, the Twins). It had hatches that could be opened in space to permit spacewalking, a major Gemini objective. Other major objectives were to practice and perfect in-orbit maneuvering; carry out rendezvous and docking with other craft; and assess the effects on men and equipment of extended periods of weightlessness on long-duration flights.

All these objectives would have to be met if Apollo was to be successful. And, one by one, on the 10 manned Gemini missions from March 1965 through November 1966, they were.

The first manned mission, Gemini 3, took place on 23 March. It was a three-orbit test flight, flown by Mercury astronaut Virgil Grissom and John Young, making his space debut in what was to be an illustrious career that spanned the Gemini, Apollo and shuttle eras. The Gemini 4 flight was highlighted by Edward White making the first American spacewalk on 3 June 1965 (as usual, he had been upstaged by Russian cosmonaut Alexei Leonov, who had spacewalked three months earlier).

In December 1965 Gemini 6 and 7 performed the first rendezvous in orbit, approaching to within 30 cm (1 foot) of one another. The Gemini 7 mission went on to break all space duration records, returning on 18 December after 14 days in orbit. On 16 March 1966 Gemini 8 made the first docking in space, with an unmanned Agena target vehicle. Making his space debut on this occasion was Neil Armstrong, destined three years later to become the first man on the Moon.

On subsequent Gemini flights the astronauts perfected the rendezvous and docking techniques, carried out spacewalks and performed a variety of experiments. They also demonstrated the great potential of orbital photography. The final mission, Gemini 12, which took place from 11-15 November 1966, encapsulated the success of the Gemini program. The astronauts carried out flawless rendezvous and docking maneuvers and individually set some very impressive records. Commander James Lovell by mission's end had logged a total of 425 hours in space. Pilot Edwin Aldrin logged a record total of 5½ hours spacewalking. The next time he set foot outside a spacecraft, it would be on the Moon.

▲ The Gemini 7 spacecraft floats into view through the hatch window of Gemini 6 during the first space rendezvous on 15 December 1965.

▶ To practice docking maneuvers the Gemini astronauts use unmanned Agena target vehicles, as here on the last Gemini mission (Gemini 12) in November 1966.

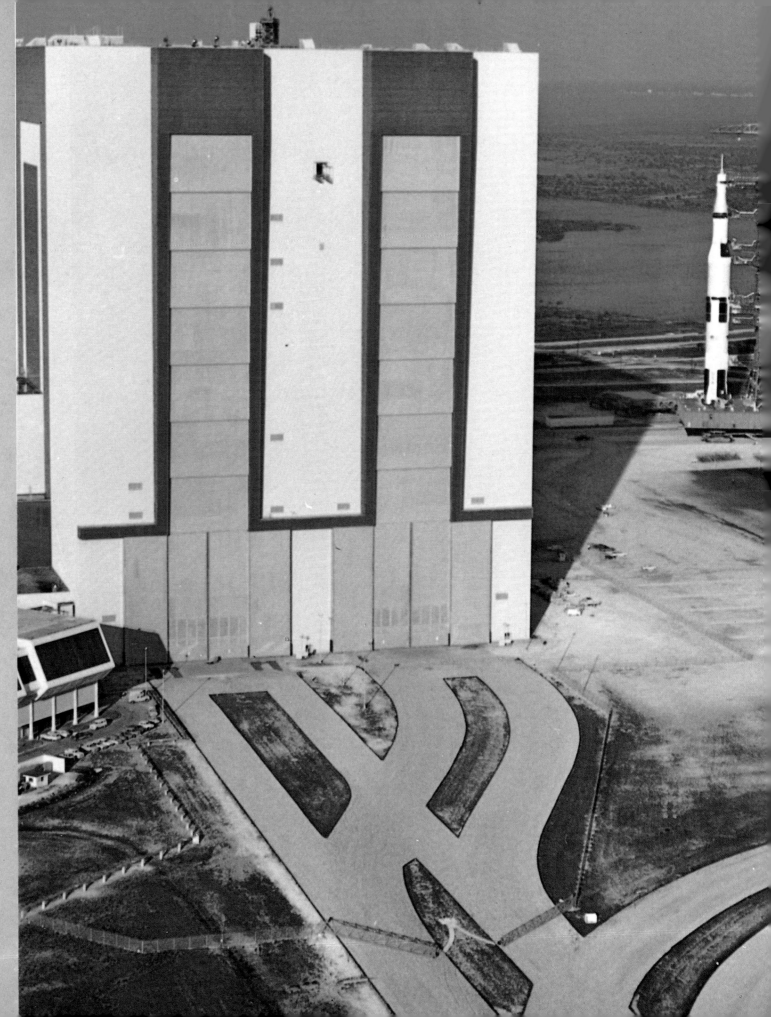

14

▶ An aerial view of Complex 39 at the Kennedy Space Center during the Apollo era, showing the massive structures the Moon shots demanded. The huge VAB dwarfs everything, even the 36-storey Saturn V.

# TWO

# Developing the Hardware

**A**T THE SAME TIME as first the Mercury and then the Gemini astronauts were performing their increasingly impressive feats in the space arena, work was forging ahead on the new technologies and new techniques, the hardware and the software that would be needed to bring the Apollo program to fruition.

There was the Apollo spacecraft itself, a three-module vehicle designed to carry a three-man crew. A modular design was demanded by the method of achieving a lunar landing – lunar orbit rendezvous. With the crew aboard, the Apollo spacecraft weighed nearly 45 tonnes (100,000 pounds).

To lift such a weight into orbit and then accelerate it to the Moon required a launch rocket of gargantuan proportions, the mighty Saturn V. Standing 36 storeys high, the Saturn V weighed 3000 tonnes (over 6 million pounds). As a NASA handout put it, Saturn V, with spacecraft attached, 'would be longer than a football field, have a base diameter greater than the combined widths of three tractor-trailer rigs, weigh more than a light Navy cruiser, and develop more power than a string of Volkswagens from New York to Seattle.'

As Saturn V, brainchild of rocket pioneer Wernher von Braun, was being developed at the Marshall Space Flight Center in Huntsville, Alabama, a mammoth new building was springing up on Merritt Island, inland from the existing launch sites at Cape Canaveral. Known as the Vehicle Assembly Building (VAB), it was to be the focus of Complex 39, the launch facility of what was soon (1963) to be the John F. Kennedy Space Center.

On 9 November 1967 the swampy wilderness that makes up much of the Space Center reverberated to the mighty roar of a Saturn V for the first time as it punched its way into the heavens. Just 13 months later another was leaping from the launch pad carrying Apollo 8 to the Moon. Ten times the Saturn V carried astronauts into space; not once did it let them down.

▲ Oddest-looking of all the Apollo hardware is the lunar module, which has a strictly functional design. This one is *Spider* (Apollo 9), pictured against a cloudy backcloth in Earth orbit in March 1969.

▶ The command module is the only part of the Apollo/Saturn V vehicle to return to Earth intact. This is the Apollo 12 craft, noticeably blackened by its searing hot re-entry into the atmosphere.

◀ The Apollo 7 command and service modules being lowered into the lunar module adapter. Afterwards the unit will be fixed atop the Saturn V launch vehicle.

### The command module: Home for the crew

Three modules made up the Apollo spacecraft. The crew were accommodated in the command module (CM). Right until the end of a mission, the CM was mated to the service module (SM). The composite unit was called the CSM (command and service modules). The third element of Apollo was the lunar module (LM), the part that ferried two of the astronauts down to the Moon's surface and back.

The CM was cone-shaped, 3.5 meters (12 feet) high, and with a base diameter of some 3.9 meters (13 feet). It was a double-walled structure, with an inner pressurized compartment; the air pressure was maintained at about one-third sea-level atmospheric pressure. The inner shell was made of an aluminum 'sandwich' with a honeycomb core; the outer shell was a stainless steel honeycomb sandwich. The curved base was covered with a reinforced plastic coating about 5 cm (2 inches) thick. This formed the heat shield, the part designed to melt and burn up during re-entry, a process known as ablation.

Inside the pressure shell were three couches for the crew. When they were strapped in their couches, the crew had their backs towards the launch rocket, the position in which they could best withstand the vicious acceleration of the Saturn V's engines. The CM had five windows – two side windows, two for rendezvous and docking, and a viewing port unit for taking sextant and telescope readings for navigation.

The main instrument panel, which extended much of the way around the inside of the module, housed most of the over 560 switches, 24 display instruments, 40 mechanical event indicators and 71 lights.

### The service module: Providing back-up

The SM was a cylinder that mated with the base of the CM and was of similar diameter. It measured 7.4 meters (24 feet) in length, about a third of which was taken up by the nozzle of its main engine, the service propulsion system (SPS).

The SM was the main equipment module, most of the bulk of

▶ With legs in the stowed position, the Apollo 10 lunar module is about to be installed in its adapter. Note the gold and silver foil, which stops the structure overheating in the sun.

which was taken up by the tanks to feed the SPS engines. The fuel was a form of hydrazine, the oxidizer was nitrogen tetroxide. No igniter was required because these propellants are hypergolic – they burst into flame the instant they mix. Two smaller tanks, of liquid oxygen and liquid hydrogen, fed the fuel cells that supplied the spacecraft with power. The water produced as a by-product of the cells provided the crew with its drinking water.

Four sets of four-nozzle jet units, the quad thrusters, were located externally on the SM. They made up the Apollo CSM's reaction control system (RCS). Different sets of nozzles were fired to maneuver the spacecraft around either of the three axes. Between them the CM and SM contained no fewer than 2,000,000 individual parts.

### The lunar module – The ferry ship

The LM, which took astronauts down to the Moon's surface and back, was the most curious looking contraption. Its odd shape was dictated not by aerodynamics or any other scientific principle, only by its function. It was of very flimsy construction, and had it been used on Earth it would probably have collapsed like a pack of cards on landing or torn itself apart when taking off. It was minimally engineered to perform in the low lunar gravity (one-sixth of the Earth's).

The LM was actually made up of two parts, an ascent stage and a descent stage, each of which had its own engine. They formed a

▶ In the 'rocket park' at the Kennedy Space Center you can appreciate the mammoth scale of the Apollo hardware. The author stands alongside a Saturn V first-stage engine in October 1988 on the 20th anniversary of the first manned mission, Apollo 7. Pictured on its side in the background is a Saturn IB, the type of vehicle used to launch Apollo 7.

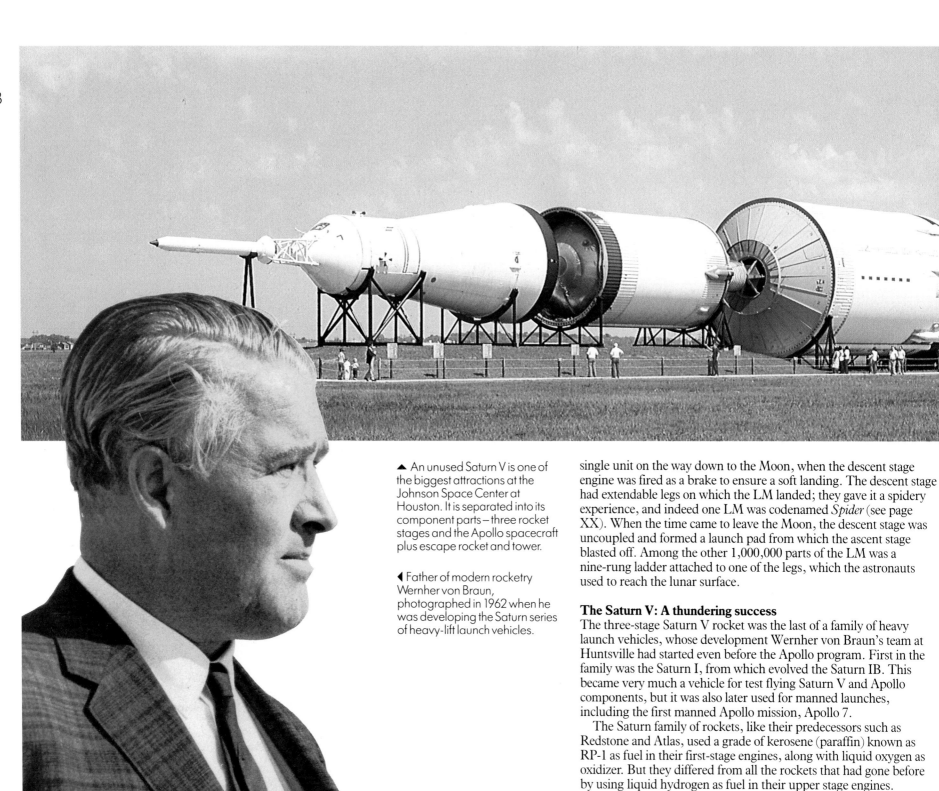

▲ An unused Saturn V is one of the biggest attractions at the Johnson Space Center at Houston. It is separated into its component parts – three rocket stages and the Apollo spacecraft plus escape rocket and tower.

◀ Father of modern rocketry Wernher von Braun, photographed in 1962 when he was developing the Saturn series of heavy-lift launch vehicles.

single unit on the way down to the Moon, when the descent stage engine was fired as a brake to ensure a soft landing. The descent stage had extendable legs on which the LM landed; they gave it a spidery experience, and indeed one LM was codenamed *Spider* (see page XX). When the time came to leave the Moon, the descent stage was uncoupled and formed a launch pad from which the ascent stage blasted off. Among the other 1,000,000 parts of the LM was a nine-rung ladder attached to one of the legs, which the astronauts used to reach the lunar surface.

## The Saturn V: A thundering success

The three-stage Saturn V rocket was the last of a family of heavy launch vehicles, whose development Wernher von Braun's team at Huntsville had started even before the Apollo program. First in the family was the Saturn I, from which evolved the Saturn IB. This became very much a vehicle for test flying Saturn V and Apollo components, but it was also later used for manned launches, including the first manned Apollo mission, Apollo 7.

The Saturn family of rockets, like their predecessors such as Redstone and Atlas, used a grade of kerosene (paraffin) known as RP-1 as fuel in their first-stage engines, along with liquid oxygen as oxidizer. But they differed from all the rockets that had gone before by using liquid hydrogen as fuel in their upper stage engines.

The Saturn V, which evolved from Saturn IB technology, dwarfed its predecessor, standing, with Apollo attached, no less than 111 metres (365 feet) tall. The first stage alone (the SIC) was as tall as the Saturn IB. Some 11 meters (33 feet) in diameter, the SIC boasted five F-1 engines, each of which had a thrust of 680,000 kg (1.5 million pounds) – the combined thrust of all eight Saturn IB engines! When

all five engines of the Saturn V roared into life on the launch pad, five turbopumps with the combined power of 30 diesel locomotives forced the propellants into the engines at the rate of three tonnes every second.

The second and third stages of the Saturn V both had liquid hydrogen engines known as J-2s. The second stage (the SII) had five engines; the third stage (the SIVB), derived from the upper stage of the Saturn IB, had a single engine. The third-stage engine, to fulfill mission requirements, had to have the capability of re-start.

In the launch configuration the Apollo CSM, with CM uppermost, sat on top of the Saturn/Apollo stack. It was attached to an escape tower, surmounted by a rocket that would pull it clear during a launch emergency. To give an idea of the scale of development from Mercury through Apollo: the escape rocket packed more thrust than the Redstone that launched Alan Shepard on the first American suborbital flight!

The LM was enclosed below the CSM within a shroud called the Saturn adapter. Below this, at the top of the SIVB rocket housing, was the instrument unit. This was the electronic brains of Apollo, an assortment of 'black boxes' for checking out rocket systems and controlling flight, together with inertial guidance equipment for keeping the vehicle on course. Three million parts combined to make the Saturn V the biggest and most powerful rocket there had ever been.

### The VAB: Hanger for a Moon rocket

To launch the mighty Saturn V required facilities that included other hardware of equally gargantuan proportions. Among the facilities required were these:

▶ Pictured together at dusk are the Moon and the Moon rocket. The Saturn V is waiting to make its unmanned maiden voyage. It lifts off on 9 November 1967 and performs flawlessly throughout the mission (Apollo 4).

A massive hanger that could accommodate four launch vehicles at once.

Movable platforms on which the launch vehicles could be assembled and transported to the launch pad.

A method of carrying the prodigiously heavy rockets on the mobile platforms.

A movable service structure (gantry) 45 storeys high to allow servicing of the launch vehicle on the pad.

A launch control center, from which countdown and launch operations would be controled.

Work began on the facilities in 1962 and continued for four years, with the expenditure of some $800 million. The result was Launch Complex 39, which became, and is still, the heart of the John F. Kennedy Space Center. The facilities and hardware have since been modified for the space shuttle era that is now upon us.

The hanger built to put together the huge Apollo stack was the Vehicle Assembly Building. This stands 160 meters (526 feet) high, 158 meters (518 feet) wide and 218 meters (716 feet) long. One of the world's biggest buildings, it encloses a volume of over 3.5 million cubic meters (130 million cubic feet) and covers an area of over 3 hectares (nearly 8 acres). From a distance the VAB does not seem overly big, because there is nothing nearby to compare it with. Only when you get up close can you appreciate its enormity.

In each of the four high bays of the VAB work platforms were installed at various levels to permit access to the various stages of the Saturn V during assembly. They were retracted against the walls when the vehicle was rolled out. The Saturn was built up stage by stage on a mobile launcher, which carried it out to the launch pads. Two identical launch pads were constructed, 39A and 39B. Both saw service in the Apollo era, and both are now in use once again for shuttle launches.

### The mobile launcher: Roll-out to the pad

The mobile launcher had a square base, about 0.2 hectare (half an acre) in area and two storeys high. In the VAB and on the launch pads the base rested on 7-meter (22-foot) high pedestals. Built within the base were insulated compartments in which mechanical, electronic and communications equipment was located, all of which could be operated remotely from the launch control center.

On the surface of the base were giant hold-down arms which gripped and restrained the launch vehicle for some 8 to 9 seconds while the first-stage engines built up to full power. Then the arms were released to allow lift-off. Immediately beneath the rocket engines a square opening allowed the searing hot exhaust gases to vent into the flame trench in the launch pad.

A red-painted steel tower, incorporating a pair of high-speed

▶ The Saturn V thunders off the launch pad with a thrust of over 3.5 million kg (7½ million pounds). This one is carrying Apollo 8, aiming to make the first circumnavigation of the Moon.

▲ This dramatic photograph, taken by an on-board camera, captures the instant of separation of the interstage section, between the first and second stages, during the second unmanned test mission of the Saturn V (Apollo 6).

◀ The first tricky part of the lunar orbit rendezvous technique is to configure the Apollo spacecraft for its translunar journey. In this operation the crew turn round the CSM and dock with the LM. Then they fire the RCS thrusters and pull away from the third stage.

▼ When Apollo reaches lunar orbit, two astronauts in the LM descend to the surface. They fire the engine of the descent stage as a brake to slow them down for a soft landing.

elevators, rose from the base of the mobile launcher to a height of 136 meters (445 feet) and was capped by a hammerhead crane. The structure carried the umbilicals – the lines feeding power and propellants to the launch vehicle. It had 17 work platforms and 9 swing arms which gave engineers access to the vehicle. The upper arm, at the 98-meter (320-foot) level, provided access to the command module and was used by the astronauts.

When carrying a Saturn V/Apollo stack, the mobile launcher weighed the best part of 6000 tonnes (13 million pounds). To transport such a weight and such an extraordinary payload demanded a unique type of vehicle. The result was a massive crawler transporter, propelled by four twin-crawler truck units, one at each corner. Each truck carried its own control cab, and their movement was synchronized by computer.

Weighing 2900 tonnes (6.3 million pounds) unloaded, the crawler transporter measured 40 meters (130 feet) long, nearly 35 meters (115 feet) wide and up to 8 meters (26 feet) high. When transporting the Saturn/Apollo stack out to the launch pad, the transporter moved at a sedate 1.6 km/h (1 mph). Because of this it was nicknamed the 'mighty tortoise'. Two of the 'mighty tortoises' were built, and they have since been renovated to carry the shuttle stacks out to the launch pads. They are still the world's largest land vehicles.

### Lunar orbit rendezvous: The way to the Moon

The technique NASA chose to achieve a Moon landing involved separation, rendezvous and docking maneuvers in lunar orbit and was known as lunar orbit rendezvous (LOR).

To see how the LOR worked, let's follow a typical lunar landing mission. The giant Saturn V/Apollo stack blasts off the pad with an awesome roar. As it ascends, it sheds in turn its first then its second stages, accelerating all the while. The third stage fires briefly, and the Apollo with third-stage still attached enters orbit about 190 km (120 miles) high. Speed 28,000 km/h (17,500 mph); mission elapsed time less than 12 minutes.

In this parking orbit around Earth the three crew members, in conjunction with Mission Control, check out all Apollo's systems and make final computations. If all is A-OK, they fire the third-stage engine again to boost their speed to over 38,500 km/h (24,000 mph) and inject them into a translunar trajectory, which will take them to the Moon.

Next come some tricky docking maneuvers. The crew separate the CSM from the third stage, turn it round and edge back to dock with the LM. Then they pull it clear. And they stay in this configuration, not under power but coasting, until after about 2½ days they reach the vicinity of the Moon. They may need to fire the SM's engine sometime on the outward leg to finely tune their trajectory so that it

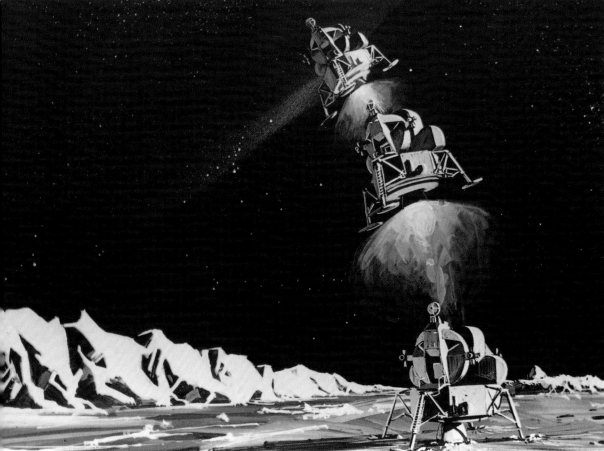

▶ After jettisoning the SM, the
astronauts in the CM slam into the
Earth's atmosphere at an
incredible 40,000 km/h (25,000
mph). The searing heat generated
by air friction makes the heat
shield at the base of the CM glow
red hot, but it does not penetrate
the cabin crew.

▼ The drag of the atmosphere
brakes the CM until it is traveling
slow enough for the parachutes to
open. They lower it to a gentle
splashdown at sea. (Here it is, the
Apollo 10 CM.)

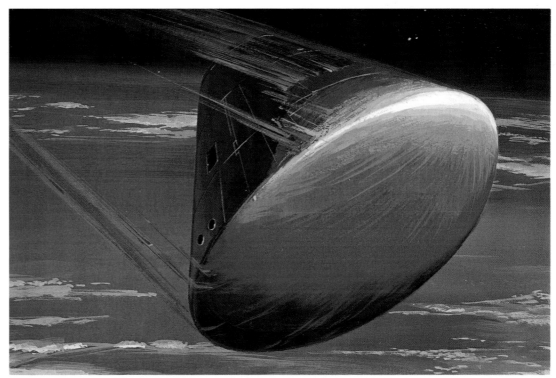

takes them to within about 100 km (62 miles) of the lunar surface.

The Moon's gravity swings them round behind the Moon. At the
appropriate time, they fire the SM's engine again as a brake to slow
them down so that they can be captured by the Moon and enter lunar
orbit.

Later, after thorough systems checks, two of the astronauts crawl
into the LM and power it up. They extend the LM's spidery landing
legs and then cut loose from the CSM. Using the LM's descent
engine as a retrobrake, they swoop down to the surface, flying the
final approach manually to avoid any hazards, such as rocks and
craters.

## Heading for home

After completing their extra-vehicular activity (EVA), the astronauts
lift off from the Moon in the ascent stage of the LM and head back
into orbit to rendezvous with the CSM, which has all the while been
orbiting above them. After docking with the CSM, they transfer to it
themselves, rock and soil samples and other equipment. The ascent
stage is then jettisoned.

To get home, they fire the SM's engine again while they are
behind the Moon. This boosts them into a transearth trajectory,
which carries them back in about three days. As they near the Earth,
its gravity makes them accelerate until, when they are about to
re-enter the atmosphere, they are traveling at speeds approaching
40,000 km/h (25,000 mph).

It is essential that they hit the atmosphere at exactly the right
angle. If the angle were too steep, they would experience too much
friction and would burn up. If the angle were too shallow, they
would 'bounce' off the atmosphere and shoot off into space with no
hope of rescue.

Just before re-entry they jettison the SM, which meets its end by
burning up like a shooting star because of air friction. The crew in
the CM, however, are protected by its heat shield. This glows red
and white hot and boils away, which is what it should do, and
prevents the near 3000°C temperatures created by air friction as the
air brakes the CM from penetrating the structure.

A few kilometers above the Earth first a drogue, then three main
parachutes open to lower the CM to a gentle splashdown at sea. This
cone, now blackened and charred, is all that remains of the behemoth
that soared from the launch pad.

▶ Russell Schweickart snaps the Apollo 9 command module from the lunar module *Spider* in March 1969. The two modules are docked together in Earth orbit during the first full flight test of the lunar module.

# THREE

**A**S THE GARGANTUAN HARDWARE was being readied for man's greatest adventure, robot space probes were being despatched to reconnoiter the lunar surface and try to establish just what it is really like. In turn Ranger, Surveyor and Lunar Orbiter probes sent back a flood of data and tens of thousands of images, which helped NASA scientists select the Apollo landing sites.

By the end of 1966 things were looking good. The lunar surveys were going well, the hardware was coming along nicely and the Gemini program had just been completed with spectacular success. But in January 1967 three astronauts scheduled to make the first manned flight in the Apollo CSM met a horrific end in a flash fire in the cockpit during training. This brought CSM testing and development to a halt while NASA investigated the cause of the catastrophe.

With the decade rapidly running out, could Apollo now reach the Moon to meet Kennedy's deadline? Although it pulled out all the stops, NASA still lost over 18 months before it was ready in October 1968 to launch into Earth orbit its modified spacecraft and the first Apollo crew. But from this mission on, designated Apollo 7, the Gods smiled favorably on the Apollo program.

In December 1968 Apollo 8 made a stunning circumnavigation of the Moon. In March 1969 Apollo 9 rocketed into Earth orbit to test-fly the whole Apollo spacecraft, CSM and LM, for the first time. And two months later Apollo 10 flew to the Moon as a complete dress rehearsal for a lunar landing – except it didn't land. How frustrating it must have been for the astronauts to swoop so tantalizingly close to the Moon's surface but not be able to land. But that honor was reserved for the crew of Apollo 11 in July.

# Blazing the Lunar Trail

▼ Surveyor 1 photographs its own shadow on the Ocean of Storms the day before lunar sunset. It soft-landed two weeks earlier, on 1 June 1966, proving that the surface is firm enough for craft to land on.

### Probing the Moon

With the Moon being Earth's neighbor in space, it was inevitable that it would be the first target for long-distance space probes. The first three American probes, Pioneers 1 to 3, launched to the Moon in 1958, never made it. It was left to the Russians to achieve the first near-miss (6000 km, 3700 miles) in January 1959 with their probe Luna (Lunik) 1. In September of that year Luna 2 was right on target, becoming the first man-made object to reach another world. Less than a month later Luna 3 performed an even greater feat by looping around the Moon and sending back pictures of its always hidden farside.

American efforts to reach the Moon with Thor-Able probes ended in dismal failure. The US initially had no luck either with its Ranger craft, designed to transmit TV pictures of the surface before crash-landing. But at last, in July 1964, Ranger 7 came up trumps. In an unaccustomed flawless mission it transmitted over 4000 close-up pictures of the Sea of Clouds (Mare Nubium). Rangers 8 and 9 followed in 1965.

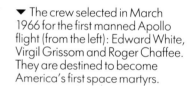

◀ The Ranger probe, which pioneers close-up surface imaging of the Moon. It takes pictures with six TV cameras before crash-landing.

▼ The crew selected in March 1966 for the first manned Apollo flight (from the left): Edward White, Virgil Grissom and Roger Chaffee. They are destined to become America's first space martyrs.

▼ The Lunar Orbiter probes take spectacular high-resolution photographs to help pinpoint suitable landing sites for the Apollo missions. They build up a picture by scanning in narrow strips. The large crater in this picture, Taruntius, is about 56 km (35 miles) across.

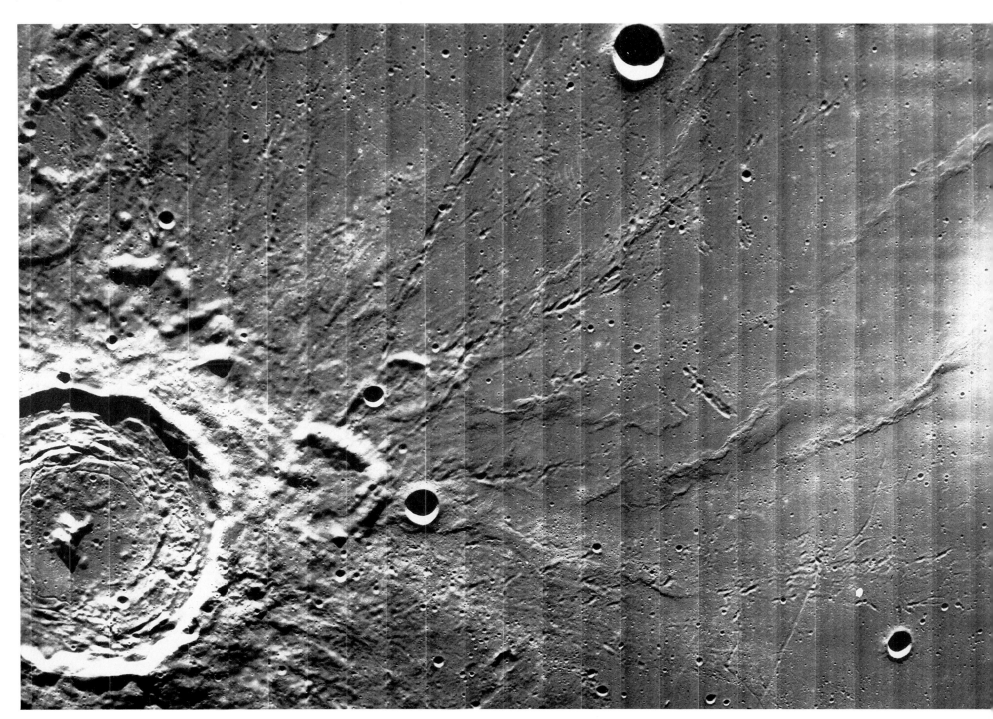

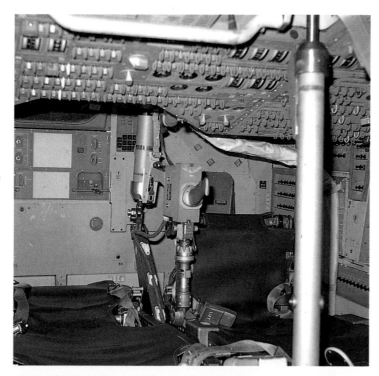

▶ The interior of the Apollo command module, viewed through the open hatch. At bottom are the astronauts' couches; above and to the sides, panels of instruments and controls.

▼ The interior of the Apollo 1 command module after the flash fire that killed astronauts Edward White, Virgil Grissom and Roger Chaffee, again viewed through the open hatch. The fire, probably caused by an electrical fault, became an inferno in seconds because of the oxygen atmosphere inside the module.

### Soft landing

NASA was also successful with the first shot in its Surveyor series, which made a perfect soft landing on the Ocean of Storms (Oceanus Procellarum) in June 1966. This came five months after the Russians had landed an instrument capsule on the surface, Luna 9. Both landings confirmed that the lunar surface was hard enough to land on. Hitherto, some authorities reckoned that the Moon might be covered in deep dust drifts that would make it impossible to land.

Launched in January 1968, Surveyor 7 brought the series of the robot-landing missions to a close. Together these spacecraft returned over 80,000 close-up pictures of the surface. They dug trenches in the soil to test its texture. They also analyzed the soil with sophisticated instruments. The results indicated that, geologically, the Earth and the Moon were not as completely different as many scientists had expected.

While the Surveyors were digging into and analyzing the lunar soil, Lunar Orbiter probes circling overhead were carrying out a comprehensive survey of the lunar surface. Launched over a 12-month period beginning in August 1966, they were outstandingly successful and photographed over 99 per cent of the Moon in high-resolution. These photographs helped NASA finalize the Apollo landing sites. Slight disturbances in the Orbiters' orbits led to the discovery of mascons, curious concentrations of mass under many of the lunar maria.

### Apollo 1: 'We're burning up!'

With Apollo hardware and software shaping up well, the first manned flight of Apollo was scheduled for February 1967. On 27 January the prime crew for the mission, Apollo 1, were taking part in a practice mission simulation in the Apollo CSM atop the launch stack on Complex 34 at Cape Kennedy. They were Mercury astronaut Virgil Grissom, Gemini spacewalker Edward White, and rookie Roger Chaffee.

They had been into the simulation for over five hours, strapped in their couches inside the far from spacious cabin. The cabin was pressurized with oxygen. Suddenly a voice crackled over the intercom: 'We've got a fire in the cockpit! ... We're burning up!' Within seconds the fire, fuelled by the pure oxygen atmosphere, became an inferno. The astronauts never stood a chance.

Grissom, White and Chaffee became America's first space martyrs. Their horrific end sent NASA back to the drawing board to redesign the Apollo CSM to ensure that such a tragedy could never happen again.

### Apollo 7: 'A magnificent flying machine'

The modified CSM was not ready for flight testing until the fall of

1968. The 11-day mission, designated Apollo 7, began on 11 October, when a Saturn IB carried aloft the CSM and its three astronauts, Walter Schirra, Donn Eisele and Walter Cunningham.

The mission was totally successful as it tested the CSM's systems and evaluated the performance of mission support facilities on the ground, through the Manned Space Flight Network of communications. The crew, who were wearing the new Apollo spacesuit, carried out rendezvous and docking maneuvers with the SIVB upper stage of their launch vehicle to simulate the operations that would on later flights be necessary to extract the lunar module. They also broadcast live telecasts from orbit, bringing space vividly into the living rooms of millions across the world for the first time.

The mission drew to a close with a perfect splashdown. Commander Schirra pronounced the Apollo CSM 'a magnificent flying machine'.

**Apollo 8: 'There is a Santa Claus'**

Apollo 8, which blasted off the launch pad just two months after Apollo 7 returned, vies with Apollo 11 as the most significant mission in space history. On 21 December it disappeared into the heavens to attempt a pioneering circumnavigation of the Moon. On board were Frank Borman, James Lovell and William Anders.

Their flawless six-day flight marked up a spectacular series of space firsts. It was the first manned Saturn V flight; the first time man had come under the influence of a gravity other than the Earth's; the first time he had traveled at speeds close to Earth-escape velocity (40,000 km/h, 25,000 mph).

Apollo 8 homed in on the Moon on Christmas Eve and, with a retroburn of the CSM's engine, entered lunar orbit and began the first of 10 circuits of the Moon some 112 km (70 miles) above its surface. The crew made two live telecasts from orbit, and earthlings 385,000 km (240,000 miles) away marveled at what they saw – the

▲ On the first manned Apollo flight in October 1968 the Apollo 7 crew practice docking with a simulated target (the white disc) inside the upper stage of the Saturn V.

▼ After 11 days in orbit, the Apollo 7 crew sport beards when they are picked up by the recovery ship USS *Essex*. From left to right they are Walter Schirra, Donn Eisele and Walter Cunningham.

◀ With their target shining palely in the early morning sky, the Apollo 8 astronauts begin their historic flight on 21 December 1968. By Christmas Eve they are circling the Moon and reading movingly from the Book of Genesis.

▼ The Apollo 8 astronauts photograph stunning lunar landscapes both on the nearside and the farside. This photograph shows the rugged cratered highlands that predominate on the farside, where there are no large maria.

barren cratered landscape, the seas and mountains, Earth rising over the lunar horizon. It was the most riveting television ever.

During one of the Christmas Eve transmissions, the crew read in turn from the Bible's Book of Genesis. The simplicity of the biblical prose and the primeval starkness of the lunar landscape combined to make this a profoundly moving experience.

On Christmas morning, as Apollo 8 swung behind the Moon on its last orbit, the crew prepared to fire the CSM's engine to kick it out of lunar orbit and back towards the Earth. Mission Control at Houston had no way of knowing whether this critical maneuver had been successful until the spacecraft reappeared around the limb of the Moon. Then the crew reported to an anxious Houston that the burn had been good. 'Please be informed,' they said, 'there is a Santa Claus!' Apollo 8 was on its way home.

The crew emerged unscathed through the final hazard, too, a searing re-entry into the Earth's atmosphere traveling at nearly 40,000 km/h (25,000 mph). NASA's Acting Administrator Thomas Paine called the flight 'one of the great pioneering efforts of mankind'. That it was.

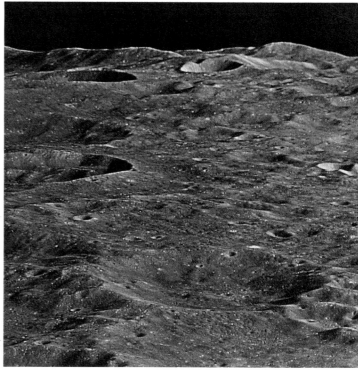

## Apollo 9: 'The friendliest Spider'

The year 1969 dawned, leaving just 12 months remaining of the decade. Could NASA meet Kennedy's deadline? The recent successes gave them confidence that they could. The Saturn V was performing brilliantly; the CSM likewise; operational procedures seemed faultless; Apollo 8's flight through lunar gravity had helped finely tune the navigation systems. The one major hurdle remaining was to check out the LM.

The LM, key to the lunar landing, had hitherto proved a headache. Not until March was it ready for its first test flight on Apollo 9. Lift-off on 3 March saw the Saturn V/Apollo vehicle in its Moon-landing configuration for the first time. The main objective of the 10-day mission was to put the LM through its paces in Earth orbit, performing the separation, rendezvous and docking maneuvers required of it during a Moon landing.

Soon after reaching orbit CSM pilot David Scott mated *Gumdrop* (codename for the CSM) with *Spider* (codename for the LM) and pulled it clear of the SIVB third stage which housed it. On the third day of the mission, Commander James McDivitt and LM pilot Russell Schweickart transferred to *Spider* for checks. But it was not until two days later that they separated and began to perform rendezvous maneuvers with *Gumdrop*. By firing *Spider*'s descent engine, they dropped over 160 km (100 miles) behind *Gumdrop* at one point where they were out of visual contact. They had to rely on radar and instruments to catch up, rendezvous and dock with the mother ship.

The LM performed like a champ. Said Scott afterwards: 'You're the biggest, friendliest, funniest-looking *Spider* I've ever seen!'

▼ On board the recovery ship USS *Yorktown* after splashdown, the Apollo 8 crew (left to right) William Anders, Frank Borman and James Lovell, receive congratulations on the telephone from US President Lyndon B. Johnson.

▲ The Apollo 8 crew receive a heroes' welcome on their return. In January 1969 crew commander Frank Borman is honored with the rare privilege of addressing a joint session of Congress in Washington DC.

**Apollo 10: 'We is down among it!'**

Any lingering doubts about the effectiveness of the Apollo hardware and software were dispelled by the flight into lunar orbit of Apollo 10, which was launched on 18 May as a full dress rehearsal for a Moon landing by Apollo 11. It was a near-flawless and spectacular mission that gave TV viewers back on Earth views of the Earth and Moon in color for the first time.

On the second day in lunar orbit, Commander Thomas Stafford and LM pilot Eugene Cernan flew *Snoopy* (the LM) away from John Young in *Charlie Brown* (the CSM) down to a breathtaking 15 km (9 miles) of the lunar surface. The objective was to fly low over the Sea of Tranquillity (Mare Tranquillitatis) to inspect and describe the site where Apollo 11 was targeted to land. As *Snoopy* skimmed over the site, Cernan reported excitedly: 'Hello Houston, we is down among it!' They had cause to be excited. No human being had ever been so close to the Moon before.

The only few moments of anxiety throughout the whole mission happened next as the two astronauts prepared to cut loose *Snoopy*'s descent stage and return to rendezvous with *Charlie Brown* orbiting above them. *Snoopy* began to gyrate because of a faulty control system. But Stafford took over manual control and the problem passed. Jettisoning the stage engine, he then fired the ascent engine and climbed to meet *Charlie Brown* for a perfect rendezvous and docking. Said Cernan wearily as he emerged after eight hours standing in *Snoopy*: 'Man, I'm glad I'm getting out!'

The flight home was uneventful. As the astronauts splashed down in the Pacific Ocean, far away in Mission Control at Houston a large sign had been put up: '51 days to launch.' It was all systems go for the great adventure, Apollo 11's lunar landing.

◀ Snapped from the window of the Apollo 9 lunar module *Spider* is the CSM *Gumdrop*. The lunar module is closing in slowly to dock, rehearsing procedures that will be needed during the early stages of the Moon flights. The 10-day flight takes place in Earth orbit in March 1969.

▼ In lunar orbit in May 1969 the crew of Apollo 10 perform the final rehearsal for the first Moon landing. Here the lunar module *Snoopy* is pictured coming into dock with the CSM *Charlie Brown*, with the rugged lunar landscape as a backcloth.

34

▶ The most famous of all space pictures, Edwin Aldrin posing for photographer Neil Armstrong during the historic first lunar landing by Apollo 11 on 20 July 1969. All around is 'magnificent desolation'.

# FOUR

EVEN AS APOLLO 10 SPLASHED DOWN on 26 May 1969 after its flawless dress-rehearsal mission, the pristine Saturn V/Apollo 11 stack was already in place on launch pad 39A at the Kennedy Space Center. A practice countdown, ending on the eve of the 4th of July, found no faults in the systems, and the decision was made to go for launch at the next available launch window, on 16 July.

After a perfect countdown, Apollo 11 left Earth on that day to attempt to land earthlings on an alien world for the first time. The honor of taking the first human step on the Moon fell on 20 July to Neil Armstrong, a 30-year-old civilian born at Wapakoneta, Ohio. As a Navy pilot he saw combat in Korea, and he was one of the famed X-15 pilots, who flew the rocket plane to the fringes of space. Like his colleagues on Apollo 11, Edwin 'Buzz' Aldrin and Michael Collins, he had first won his space wings in Gemini.

From beginning to end the Apollo 11 mission was a triumph. NASA had met the seemingly impossible challenge of landing a man on the Moon before the decade was out and returning them safely to the Earth. For good measure it repeated the feat before the decade ran its course, launching Apollo 12 in November. On that mission the astronauts started the first in-depth studies of the lunar environment.

The Apollo 13 mission in April 1970 proved indeed to be an unlucky thirteenth. The astronauts were fortunate to escape with their lives when their spacecraft was crippled by an explosion on the third day out from Earth. Only by using the LM as a lifeboat were they able to survive. An inquest into the near-disaster delayed the next attempt at a lunar landing until the following January. But with this mission, Apollo 14, there were no problems.

The Apollo program triumphantly reached its mid-course. Data was flooding in faster than scientists could cope with it; the geologists in particular were having a field day.

# 'The Eagle Has Landed'

▼ After walking on the Moon for two and a half hours, Neil Armstrong is safely back inside the lunar module, weary but triumphant. He and Edwin Aldrin have taken the 'small steps' that represent the 'giant leap for mankind'.

▲ The Apollo 11 astronauts. Mission Commander Neil Armstrong was born in Wapakoneta, Ohio, in 1931. CSM pilot Michael Collins was born in Rome, Italy, in 1931. LM pilot Edwin 'Buzz' Aldrin was born in Montclair, New Jersey, in 1930.

## Apollo 11: The adventure begins

Launch day for the historic mission of Apollo 11, 16 July 1969, dawned fair and hot. The 28-hour countdown to a 9.32 EDT (Eastern Daylight Time) lift-off was entering its final stages – no hitches. For days past 3500 newsmen from around the world had been descending on the Kennedy Space Center. People in their thousands had been flocking to vantage points along the Banana River and the beaches around Cape Kennedy to witness man's first attempt to conquer the Moon. By now they totaled upwards of a million.

Flight crew director, astronaut Donald Slayton, woke Apollo 11 commander Neil Armstrong, LM pilot Buzz Aldrin and CSM pilot Michael Collins at 4.15 am. After a steak and eggs breakfast they suited up and traveled to launch pad 39A. Riding the elevator to the top of the Saturn V, they entered the cramped CM just before 7.00 am. It was to be their home for the next eight days. By 8.32 am the access hatch had been shut, the cabin pressurized and tested for leaks, and the closeout crew were departing. The astronauts were on their own, atop the mightiest rocket there had ever been, about to go where no man had gone before.

## 'The time had come'

Afterwards Armstrong summed-up what was running through the astronauts' minds as they lay on their couches waiting for the rocket engines to ignite beneath them:

'All was ready. Everything had been done. Projects Mercury and Gemini. Seven years of project Apollo. The work of more than 300,000 Americans. Six previous unmanned and manned Apollo flights. Planning, testing, analysing, training. The time had come.

'We had a great deal of confidence. We had confidence in our hardware. The Saturn rocket, the command module and the lunar module. All flight segments had been flown on the earlier Apollo flights with the exception of the descent to and the ascent from the Moon's surface and, of course, the exploration work on the surface. These portions were far from trivial, however, and we had concentrated our training on them.

'Months of simulation with our colleagues in the Mission Control Center had convinced us that they were ready.

'Although confident, we were certainly not over confident. In research and in exploration, the unexpected is always expected. We were not overly concerned with our safety, but we would not be surprised if a malfunction or an unforeseen occurrence prevented a successful lunar landing.

'As we ascended in the elevator to the top of the Saturn on the morning of 16 July 1969, we knew that hundreds of thousands of Americans had given their best effort to give us this chance. Now it was time for us to give our best.' That they did.

## 'Godspeed'

T-5 minutes and counting, and the Apollo access arm retracts. Inside Kennedy Launch Control Center, launch director Rocco Petrone and his 463-man team monitor the final minutes of the countdown. Also present are NASA Administrator Thomas Paine, Apollo program chief Lieutenant-General Sam Phillips, and Wernher von Braun, the father of modern rocketry and designer of the Saturn V.

Within seconds of the targeted lift-off time 9.32 am, Saturn V's

five rocket engines roar to life. For two seconds the engines build up thrust. Then the hold-down clamps are released and Apollo 11 is on its way. Radios Launch Control to the crew: 'Good luck and Godspeed.' Replies Armstrong: 'Thank you very much. We know this will be a good flight.'

The 36-storey rocket begins to rise from the pad, emerging from the fireball of its engine exhausts with the power of 180 million horses. Thundering shock waves ripple over the flat Floridan landscape and blast the ears of the awestruck spectators.

'Lift-off! We have lift-off!' blare the loudspeakers. 'Go, baby, go!' someone shouts. A million people at the Cape and hundreds of millions more watching on television collectively will Apollo 11 into the heavens with whoops, yells, prayers and tears.

◀ Apollo 11 lifts off the launch pad on 16 July 1969 destination Moon. In less than 15 minutes the astronauts will be in orbit.

▼ Speeding towards the Moon, the Apollo 11 astronauts snapped this picture of their home planet, shining colorfully in the inky blackness of space. Most of northern Europe is shrouded in cloud, but northern and southern Africa and the Middle East are clear.

▲ An estimated 500 million TV viewers on Earth watch as Neil Armstrong steps down on to the lunar surface on 20 July 1969. NASA has landed a man on the Moon before the decade is out.

▶ Armstrong's boots make clear footprints in the soft lunar soil. His footprints are still there today; there is no weather to disturb them.

## 'No substitute for being there'

*16 July, 9.44 am:* Apollo 11, with third-stage rocket still attached, enters Earth orbit. At 12.22 pm, midway on its second orbit, the third-stage engine fires again to boost Apollo's speed to 38,700 km/h (24,200 mph) and kick it out of Earth orbit into a translunar trajectory. At 12.49 pm the crew begin the docking maneuvers to configure the CSM (codenamed *Columbia*) and LM (*Eagle*) for the outbound flight. The third stage is then fired again to remove it from Apollo's path.

*18 July, 11.12 pm:* Apollo, braked by Earth's gravitational pull, has slowed down to just under 3300 km/h (2060 mph). But now, only 62,500 km (38,900 miles) from the Moon, it begins to succumb to lunar gravity and starts accelerating.

*19 July, 1.28 pm:* While Apollo is out of radio contact behind the Moon, *Columbia*'s engine makes a six-minute burn to brake the craft so that it enters lunar orbit. A short second burn at 5.44 pm stabilizes the orbit between 100 and 120 km (62 and 75 miles) high above the surface.

Reports Armstrong from lunar orbit: 'We're getting this first view of the landing approach … the pictures and maps brought back by Apollos 8 and 10 give us a very good preview of what to look at here. It looks very much like the pictures, but like the difference between watching a real football game and watching it on TV – no substitute for actually being here.'

## Lunar landfall

*20 July, 9.27 pm:* LM pilot Aldrin crawls into *Eagle* and starts to power it up, followed an hour later by Armstrong. At 1.46 pm *Eagle* separates from *Columbia*. Now behind the Moon and out of radio contact with Mission Control at Houston, *Eagle*'s crew fire its descent engine, and the LM begins to drop out of orbit. At 3.47 pm an anxious Mission Control receives a report from Collins as *Columbia* emerges from behind the Moon that *Eagle* is on its way down: 'Everything's going just swimmingly. Beautiful!'

*20 July, 4.05 pm:* Armstrong throttles up the descent engine to brake the LM for landing on the Sea of Tranquillity. Seeing that they are approaching a large rock-strewn crater, Armstrong takes over manual control and steers the LM to a safer spot. His pulse rate races from its normal 77 to 156.

Aldrin calls out the altitude readings: '75 feet. Things looking good. Lights on. Picking up some dust. 30 feet. 2½ down. Faint shadow. Four forward. Four forward, drifting to the right a little. Contact light. Okay, engine stop.'

*20 July, 4.18 pm:* With only 30 seconds of fuel remaining for its engine, the LM touches down. 'We copy you down *Eagle*,' radios

▼ A rare picture taken by an automatic camera that shows both Apollo 11 astronauts on the Moon together. They are erecting the US flag, stiffened so that it can fly. Note the dramatic late lunar evening shadows.

▶ It is Edwin Aldrin's turn to step down from the descent ladder on to the Moon. The backpack he wears houses the portable life-support system to supply his spacesuit with oxygen, power and cooling water.

Mission Control. Reports Armstrong: 'Houston, Tranquillity Base here. The *Eagle* has landed.' Replies Mission Control: 'Roger Tranquillity. We copy you on the ground. You got a bunch of guys about to turn blue. We're breathing again. Thank's a lot!'

Aldrin, looking out of the LM window, describes the lunar surface: 'Looks like a collection of just about every variety of shapes, angularities and granularities, every variety of rock you could find .... It's pretty much without color. It's gray .... Some of the surface rocks ... disturbed by the rocket engine ... display a very dark gray interior and it looks like it could be country basalt.' Lunar surface science begins.

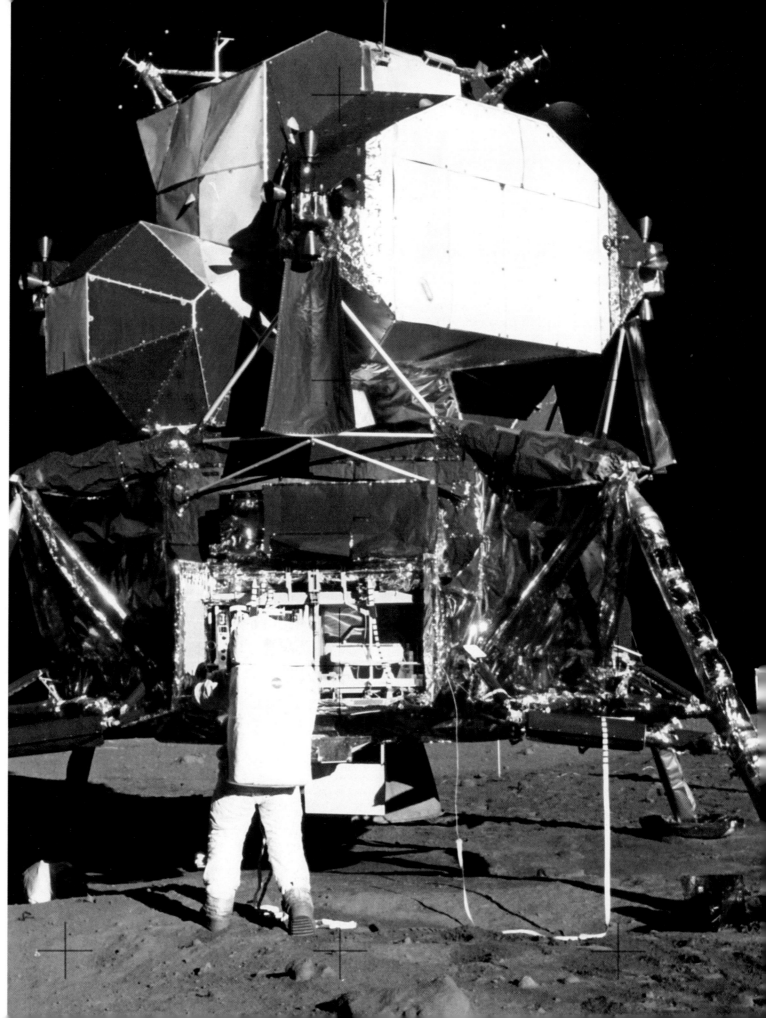

▶ Apollo 11 LM *Eagle* on the Sea of Tranquillity. Edwin Aldrin is working at the scientific equipment bay.

▶ After an uneventful flight home, the Apollo 11 crew splash down in the Pacific on 24 July 1969. They don their cover-all biological isolation garments as a precaution to prevent possible transmission of Moon germs.

▼ President Richard Nixon is on board the recovery ship USS *Hornet* to welcome home the Apollo crew. They are isolated in the mobile quarantine facility, a precaution against possible Moon germs. From left to right they are Neil Armstrong, Michael Collins and Edwin Aldrin.

## The giant leap

*20 July, 10.39 pm:* Armstrong opens *Eagle*'s hatch and, decked out for EVA with cumbersome spacesuit and backpack, squeezes through the opening on to the platform outside. Then he moves slowly down the ladder. At the last rung, he pauses.

*20 July, 10.56 pm:* Armstrong plants his left foot on the lunar surface. An estimated 500 million people, about one-fifth of the world's population, are watching 385,000 km (240,000 miles) away. Radios Armstrong: 'That's one small step for a man, one giant leap for mankind.'

The dream of the inhabitants of planet Earth throughout the ages has become reality. A human being has set foot on another world.

Armstrong gingerly moves away from the LM, testing the alien low-gravity environment. 'The surface is fine and powdery,' he says. 'I can pick it up loosely with my toe. It does adhere in fine layers like powdered charcoal to the soles and sides of my boots. I only go in … maybe an eighth of an inch, but I can see the footprints of my boots and the treads in the fine particles. There seems to be no difficulty in moving around as we suspected. It's even easier than the simulations.'

At 11.11 pm Aldrin joins Armstrong on the surface. 'Beautiful, beautiful, beautiful,' he marvels, 'a magnificent desolation.' Then the two lunarnauts carry out their prearranged workload, collecting 21 kg (46 pounds) of rock and soil samples. They set up three experiments: a 'window shade' to sample the solar wind, a laser reflector and a seismometer to measure ground tremors, or 'moonquakes'. They also plant a US flag, suitably stiffened to 'fly'. And they talk to President Richard Nixon at the White House.

*21 July, 1.11 am:* Armstrong and Aldrin are back in *Eagle* and the hatch is closed. The first manned walk on the Moon is over. At 1.54 pm the ascent stage of *Eagle* blasts off the surface to dock some 3½ hours later with *Columbia*. The moonwalkers leave behind on the Sea of Tranquillity human footprints, cameras, tools, experiments and the descent stage of the LM.

Fixed to one leg is a plaque that records for posterity Apollo 11's quantum leap into the unknown. It reads: 'Here men from planet Earth first set foot on the Moon. July 1969 AD. We came in peace for all mankind.'

## 'The greatest week in history'

*22 July, 12.56 am:* *Columbia*'s engine fires while the craft is behind the Moon. Emerging over the lunar horizon, the astronauts report that the burn is good. They are on their way home.

*24 July, 12.21 pm:* The astronauts jettison the SM. Fourteen minutes later the CM slams into the atmosphere traveling at nearly 11

◀ It seems that the whole of New York turns out on 13 August 1969 to give the Apollo 11 heroes the largest ticker-tape parade in its history.

▶ With its landing legs deployed, the Apollo 12 lunar module *Intrepid* has separated from the CSM *Yankee Clipper* and is dropping from orbit, aiming for landfall on the Ocean of Storms, just four months after Apollo 11.

▼ Here on the Ocean of Storms one of the Apollo 12 astronauts is setting up the first ALSEP scientific station. All around, the landscape is flat and featureless and covered in sticky dust.

▶ The Apollo 12 astronauts touch down within walking distance of the Surveyor 3 probe, which had landed in 1967. During their second moonwalk, the Apollo 12 astronauts examine the probe and cut pieces from it to take back to Earth for analysis.

km (7 miles) a second. For a quarter of an hour there is a radio blackout. Then contact is re-established. The crew are over their last major obstacle and splash down at 12.51 pm, 195 hours, 18 minutes and 35 seconds since they left Earth atop the Saturn V.

At 1.20 pm the astronauts emerge from the CM in their biological isolation suits and are sprayed with disinfectant against possible Moon 'germs'. Thirty-seven minutes later a helicopter whisks them to the recovery ship USS *Hornet*, where they enter the mobile quarantine trailer to begin a three-week quarantine period.

President Nixon is on hand to greet them: 'This is the greatest week in the history of the world,' he enthused. 'As a result of what you have done, the world's never been closer together .... We can reach for the stars just as you have reached so far for the stars.'

**Apollo 12: 'A veritable feast'**
Apollo 11 had proved that it could be done and that astronauts could perform efficiently in the lunar environment. Now it was time to begin to capitalize scientifically on the Apollo experience.

On 14 November 1969 Apollo 12 blasted off amidst lightning bolts and headed for the Ocean of Storms. Aboard were Commander Charles ('Pete') Conrad, LM pilot Alan Bean and CSM pilot Richard Gordon. They were aiming for lunar landfall by the Surveyor 3 probe that had landed 31 months earlier. Thanks to a tightening of landing procedures following Apollo 11's wayward touchdown – it was 7.5 km (4.5 miles) off course – Conrad flew the LM *Intrepid* down to a pinpoint landing within 185 meters (600 feet) of the probe. The astronauts later snipped off pieces of Surveyor to take back home for analysis.

However, the main tasks of lunarnauts Conrad and Bean, who went about their work in the utmost high spirits, were to collect rocks and soil, bore into the ground for core samples and set up an automatic scientific station that would continue to send back data when they left. The instruments they set up made up what was called the ALSEP (Apollo surface experiments package). They were powered by a nuclear battery called SNAP (space nuclear auxiliary power) 27.

The instruments included a magnetometer to detect any lunar magnetism, particle detectors and a seismometer. When Conrad and Bean had rejoined Gordon in the CSM *Yankee Clipper*, they sent *Intrepid* crashing to the surface at 8000 km/h (5000 mph) to give scientists back on Earth a means of calibrating the seismometer.

When the 34 kg (75 pounds) of samples were examined when Apollo 12 returned to Earth after its 10-day mission, geologists were astounded at the variety of rocks the astronauts had collected. One called them 'a veritable feast', compared with Apollo 11's samples .

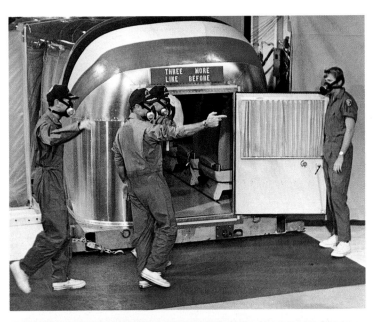

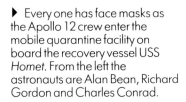

▶ Every one has face masks as the Apollo 12 crew enter the mobile quarantine facility on board the recovery vessel USS *Hornet*. From the left the astronauts are Alan Bean, Richard Gordon and Charles Conrad.

▼The crippled service module of Apollo 13, the mission that came within a whisker of being a disaster in April 1970.

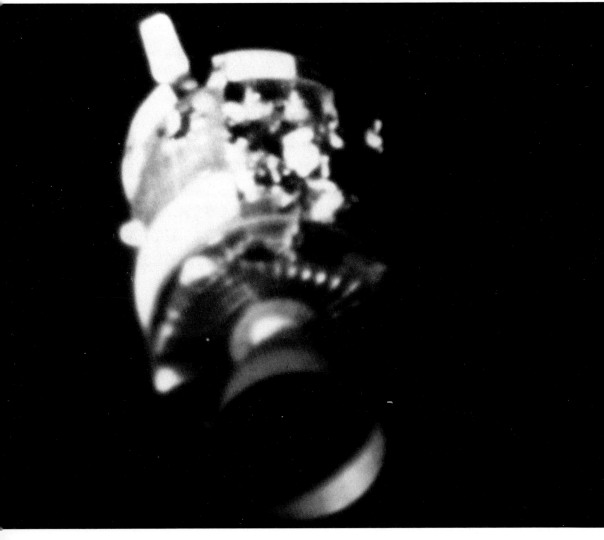

▶ (Opposite) Apollo 13 astronaut John Swigert demonstrates a makeshift air purifier the crew has rigged up to purge suffocating carbon dioxide from the spacecraft cabin.

## Apollo 13: A successful failure

On 11 April 1970 Apollo 13 blasted off, aiming to land in the foothills of the Fra Mauro formation on the Ocean of Storms. Everything went according to the textbook until the third day of the mission, when Apollo was some 320,000 km (200,000 miles) from home. The crew had just completed a telecast. CSM pilot John Swigert was in the CSM *Odyssey*, LM pilot Fred Haise was in the LM *Aquarius*, and Commander James Lovell was in between.

Suddenly they heard a 'pretty large bang'. Swigert in *Odyssey* heard an alarm go and witnessed a power loss. He radioed Mission Control: 'Hey, we've got a problem here!'

Indeed they had. An explosion had ruptured the liquid oxygen tank in the SM, knocking out its propulsion engine and cutting off the supply of power and life-supporting oxygen to *Odyssey*. There was a battery pack in *Odyssey* with a life of 10 hours, but this had to be reserved for landing. In any case Apollo was up to 90 hours from home.

There was only one option open to the crew: use the only part of Apollo that still functioned – that is, *Aquarius* – as a lifeboat. Back on Earth NASA feverishly calculated whether a return mission was possible using the oxygen and power in the LM to sustain the crew and carry out the maneuvers necessary to return them safely to Earth. On paper it worked – just. In practice, few would have betted on it.

However, work it did. But to conserve power the crew had to endure temperatures only a few degrees above freezing, which often made sleep impossible. They were, said Lovell afterwards, 'as cold as frogs in a frozen pond'. But they were alive.

On 17 April Apollo was heading towards the Earth's atmosphere. The crew first cut loose the SM and saw what havoc the explosion had caused. Then they jettisoned *Aquarius*, which had kept all three of them alive for 95 hours; it was designed to support only two men for 50 hours. As the LM floated away, Mission Control radioed: 'Farewell *Aquarius* and we thank you.' Said Lovell: 'She was a good ship.'

Soon the agony was over. The CM made a pinpoint splashdown. As NASA put it later: 'Apollo 13 must officially be classed as a failure, the first in 22 manned flights. But in another sense, as a brilliant demonstration of the human capability under almost unbearable stress, it has to be the most successful failure in the annals of space flight.'

Said President Nixon when welcoming home the astronauts: 'You did not reach the Moon, but you reached the hearts of millions of people on Earth.'

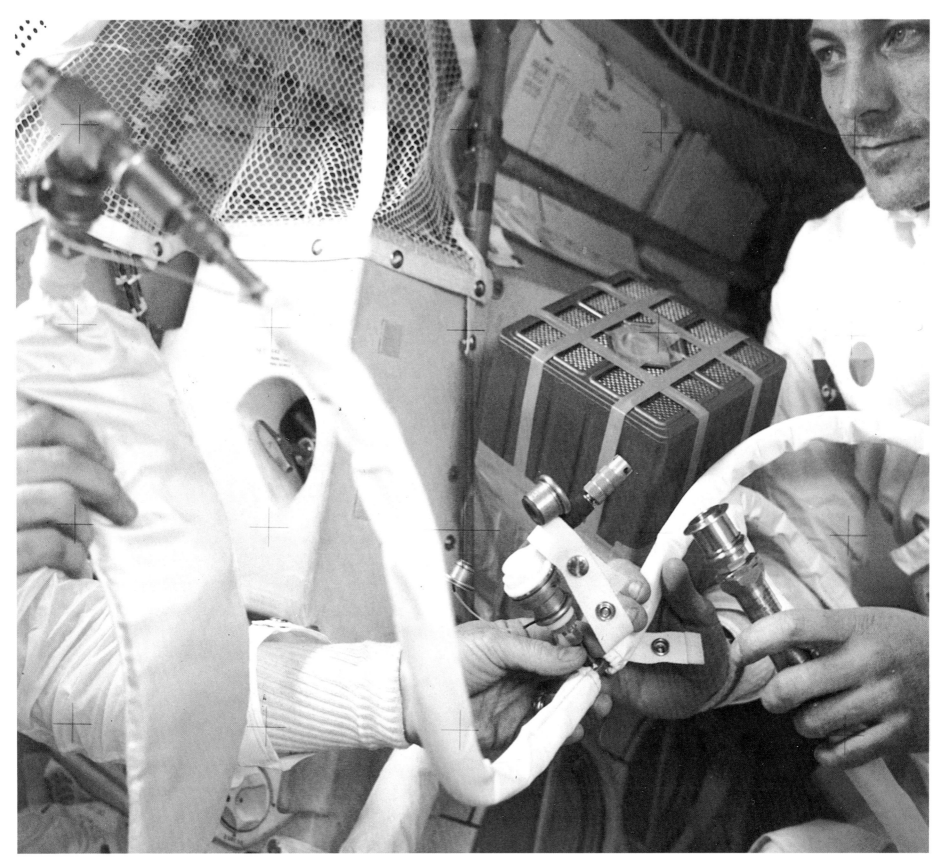

▼ The Apollo 14 moonwalkers use a modularized equipment transporter, or 'golf cart', to carry the tools they need to test and sample the soil. The astronaut here is Alan Shepard.

## Apollo 14: A lunar driver

Following Apollo 13's near-catastrophe, certain modifications were made to the Apollo CSM to prevent a recurrence of the problem. This delayed the next mission until 31 January 1971. On that day Apollo 14 headed once more for the Fra Mauro formation, and this time there were no glitches.

Having left the CM *Kitty Hawk* in lunar orbit with Stuart Roosa on board, the LM *Antares* touched down without incident at Fra Mauro near the 350-meter (1150-foot) diameter Cone crater. Moonwalkers Alan Shepard and Edgar Mitchell carried out a demanding schedule on two EVAs. For Shepard, at 47 the 'old man of space', it was a personal triumph. He made America's first suborbital flight in a Mercury capsule in 1961, only to be grounded for the next eight years with an ear infection. 'It's been a long way,' he murmured as he stepped out of *Antares*, 'but we're here.'

The two lunarnauts set up another ALSEP station, and gathered 45 kg (96 pounds) of rock and soil samples. They roamed about the lunar surface for a total of nearly 9½ hours. To carry their equipment they had what NASA euphemistically called a modularized equipment transporter (MET), which looked not unlike a golf cart.

As if to press home the similarity, at the end of the second EVA, Shepard surprised Mission Control by fitting the head of a golf club to the handle of a geological tool and producing two golf balls from his spacesuit. Swinging one-handedly, he muffed his first shot, but succeeded with his second. 'There it goes,' he said, 'miles and miles.' In truth, he admitted afterwards, his best shot actually went about 360 meters (400 yards).

◀ Thankful to be back on Earth and lucky to be alive, the Apollo 13 crew exit the recovery helicopter and board USS *Iwo Jima* on 17 April 1970. From the left they are Fred Haise, James Lovell and John Swigert.

▶ The harsh sunlight reflects from the foil-covered surface of the Apollo 14 lunar module *Antares*. The landscape here at Fra Mauro is more undulating than at the two previous landing sites.

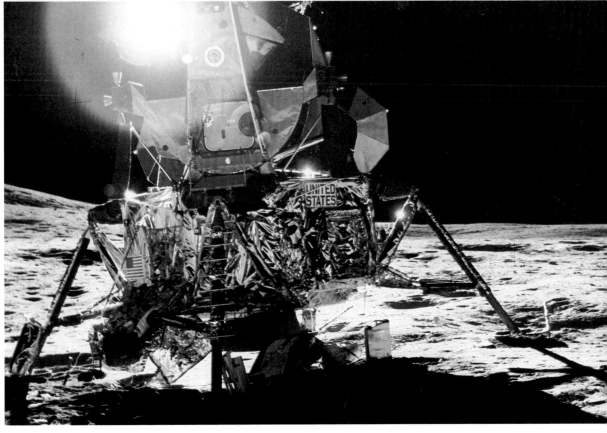

▶ Apollo 15 astronaut James Irwin salutes the US flag in this classic Apollo picture. Behind the lunar module *Falcon* is the Apennine peak Mount Hadley. At right is the astronauts' hot rod, the invaluable lunar rover.

# FIVE

A POLLO 14 saw lunar exploration really getting into its stride. Even more ambitious goals were set for the final three Moon shots, Apollo 15 through 17, and they were achieved. On each mission the astronauts made three EVAs. They set up more ALSEP stations. Up in lunar orbit the CSMs conducted extensive instrumental and photographic surveys from their scientific instrument module (SIM) bay. Apollo 15 and 16 launched subsatellites around the Moon to acquire data about the lunar environment over a longer period.

On all three missions the moonwalkers were able to cover much greater distances than their predecessors, thanks to the remarkable lunar roving vehicle, nicknamed the rover or Moon buggy. It had four-wheel drive by electric motors on each wheel. Developed at a cost of some $40 million, it had a top speed of about 16 km/h (10 mph).

On the earlier missions the LMs had set down on mare regions, with generally flat and featureless topography. The last three missions set down in the most dramatic landscapes. In July 1971 Apollo 15 landed in the foothills of the Apennine mountains at the edge of the Sea of Showers. In April 1972 Apollo 16 headed for the lunar highlands around Descartes crater. In December 1972 Apollo 17 landed in Taurus-Littrow, a rugged valley sandwiched between high massifs at the edge of the Sea of Serenity.

With Apollo 17, the Moon landings came to an end. Men from planet Earth left the Moon for the last time this century on 14 December 1972. A plaque fixed to one of the legs of the LM descent stage that still stands at Taurus-Littrow records the finale of one of the most remarkable periods in the history of exploration. It reads: 'Here man completed his first exploration of the Moon, December 1972. May the spirit of peace in which we came be reflected in the lives of all mankind.'

# Lunar Roving

▼ Eugene Cernan takes the lunar rover for a test-drive at the beginning of the first Apollo 17 EVA. By mission's end the rover will have transported him and fellow moonwalker Harrison Schmitt 35 km (22 miles).

▲ This mosaic of photographs, taken by James Irwin, form a 360° panorama of the Apollo 15 landing site, close to the foothills of the Apennine mountains. It features, from the left, part of the ALSEP scientific station; astronaut David Scott; the prominent peaks Mount Hadley and Mount Hadley Delta and between them more distant peaks of the Apennines.

## Apollo 15: 'Absolutely mind-boggling'

Billed as 'the most scientific lunar mission yet', Apollo 15 lifted off on 26 July 1971 heading for a particularly interesting site at the edge of the Sea of Showers (Mare Imbrium), between the towering Apennine mountains and the canyon-like Hadley rille. The site was chosen because it allowed sampling of a mare basin, mountains and a rille, all in one mission.

Compared with previous crews, that of Apollo 15 was not very talkative on the outward leg of the journey. Not until Apollo entered lunar orbit did things change. Commander David Scott, looking down at the lunar landscape, could not contain his excitement: 'I'll tell you, this is absolutely mind-boggling up here,' he said. 'When you get it all at once, it is absolutely overwhelming.'

Scott set down the LM *Falcon* just about 800 meters (half a mile) from target on 30 July. Later he put his head out of the top hatch and described the view: 'All the features around here are very smooth. The tops of the mountains are rounded off. There are no jagged peaks or large boulders apparent anywhere.'

The next morning Scott and LM pilot James Irwin prepared for their first EVA. Scott paused a while at the foot of the ladder to look around. 'As I stand out here in the wonders of unknown at Hadley,' he said, 'I sort of realize there's a fundamental truth to our nature. Man must explore. And this is exploration at its greatest.'

### 'A rock-and-roll ride'

The first part of the EVA was devoted to putting the lunar roving vehicle through its paces. Afterwards, they deployed the ALSEP instruments. The rover was a collapsible contraption, stowed folded on the side of the LM. Pulling a lanyard caused it to fall to the ground and unfold.

As the astronauts took it for a 'road test', driver Scott reported: 'The rover handles quite well. It negotiates small craters quite well, only there's quite a lot of roll. It feels like we need the seatbelts, doesn't it Jim? Oh, this is really a rock-and-roll ride, isn't it? Never been on a ride like this before. Oh boy!' They were clearly reveling in their new set of wheels.

During the second EVA the astronauts ventured out to the foothills of the 4500-meter (15,000-foot) high Apennine mountains. Among the rocks they gathered in their 24 bags of samples was one that caused Scott to exclaim: 'Guess what we just found? I think we found what we came for!' It was a crystalline rock, which came to be called the Genesis rock, since it was thought it might date back to the formation of the solar system. Another oddity, dubbed the Green clod, was made up of tiny spheres of green glass.

The third EVA took Scott and Irwin to Hadley rille, a meandering canyon about 1.6 km (1 mile) wide and from 180-360 km (600-1200 feet) deep. In the walls of the rille they could see lunar bedrock exposed and layers marking successive flows of lava, which suggested that the rille might have been a channel through which lava poured out of the Sea of Showers when it was formed.

### On falling bodies

On returning to base, Scott performed another impromptu experiment before the TV camera. 'Well, in my left hand I have a feather, and in my right hand a hammer. I guess one of the reasons we got here today was because of a gentleman named Galileo a long time ago, who made a rather significant discovery about falling objects in gravity fields. And we thought that where would be a better place to confirm his findings than on the Moon …. I'll drop the two of them here and hopefully they'll hit the ground at the same time.'

The heavy hammer and the light feather hit the ground together. On the Moon there was no air resistance to slow the feather's fall. 'How about that,' cried Scott, 'Mr Galileo was correct.'

When the time came for the astronauts to leave the Moon, the rover had clocked up 28 km (17½ miles) during the three days of EVAs. But its job was not quite over. The astronauts parked it so that its Earth-controlled TV camera could watch *Falcon* lift off from the Moon. The lift-off was spectacular, creating a shower of sparks and kicking up cascades of dust.

After Scott and Irwin had rejoined the third member of the crew, Alfred Worden, in CSM *Endeavour*, *Falcon* was sent crashing to the

◀ The moment of splashdown for the Apollo 15 command module as the three main parachutes lower them gently into the Pacific on 7 August 1971. Unlike previous missions the astronauts, James Irwin, David Scott and Alfred Worden, do not go into quarantine. Scientists are now satisfied that there are no germs on the Moon.

▶ The Apollo 16 astronauts explore the Descartes highlands. Here, Charles Duke is working near Plum crater, boring into the soil to extract a core sample.

surface to test the seismometers at the three ASLEP stations now functioning. On the way back home Worden came briefly into the limelight as he made the first ever deep-space walk to retrieve film canisters from the SIM bay.

### Apollo 16: Into the highlands

High-resolution photographs taken by Apollo 14 provided vital data in the selection of the landing site for Apollo 16. This was located in the lunar highlands, the light-colored portions of the Moon that we see from Earth. The target was a rolling rock-strewn plain just north of the Descartes crater and close to a formation known as Cayley. It was located at an altitude some 2400 meters (8000 feet) higher than the Apollo 11 base on the Sea of Tranquillity.

Apollo 16 began its journey to the lunar highlands on 16 April 1972. The outbound leg was marred by niggling systems faults. But more serious problems developed after Thomas Mattingly in CSM

*Casper* separated from John Young and Charles Duke in LM *Orion*, prior to *Orion* descending to the Moon. As Mattingly checked out *Casper*'s engine, he felt the spacecraft vibrate. Since the astronauts relied on this engine to get back home, it was a potentially dangerous situation. The Moon landing was postponed for six hours until checks suggested that the situation was not life-threatening. The LM went on to make a perfect landing. 'Old Orion is finally here, Houston,' reported Duke.

On this mission too, the rover served the astronauts well. It carried them for some 27 km (17 miles) during their three EVAs, which lasted over 20 hours. On the first EVA they prepared the rover and deployed the ALSEP experiments. Their second EVA took them some 5 km (3 miles) south of the landing site to a hill called Stone mountain, and their third an equal distance north to North Ray crater. They found this crater an awesome sight, over 1.2 km (0.75 mile) across and more than 200 meters (650 feet) deep.

◀ Apollo 16 moonwalker John Young is pictured with the ALSEP experiments that make up the third automatic scientific station set up so far on the Moon.

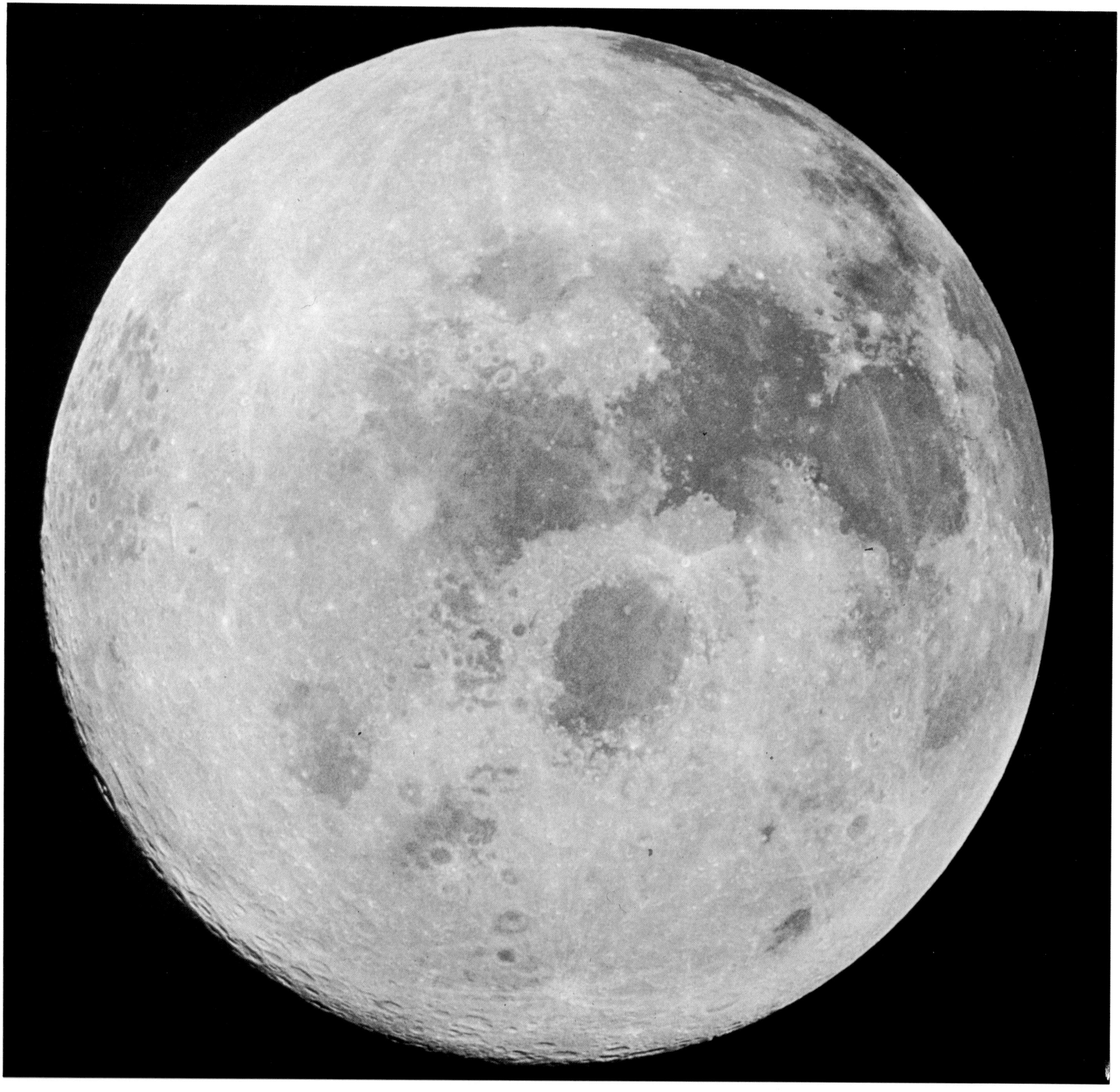

◀ The Apollo 16 astronauts photograph the full Moon as they make their way back home. But it is not the full Moon we see from Earth (compare page 62). The three large adjoining here are (from the left) Fecunditatis, Tranquillitatis maria and Serenitatis (Fertility, Tranquillity and Serenity). The circular mare below center is Mare Crisium (Sea of Crises)

◀ John Young takes this picture of the Earth with a special ultraviolet camera. It shows a surrounding halo of hydrogen gas. The spike at lower right shows where displays of aurora (southern lights) are taking place over the South Pole.

▼ The Apollo 16 astronauts are welcomed aboard the recovery ship USS *Ticonderoga* shortly after splashdown on 27 April 1972. Commander John Young is at the microphone.

They collected rock samples from around the crater rim which, as expected, proved to be bedrock thrown up by the meteorite impact that excavated the crater. These formed part of a haul of some 97 kg (213 pounds) of rock and soil samples they took back to Earth. The lunar EVAs accomplished all they had set out to, and more. But the gremlins that had plagued the mission had not gone away. Young accidentally kicked a wire loose at the ALSEP station and knocked out the heat-flow experiment, the setting-up of which had taken a great deal of their precious EVA time.

Then the three astronauts were back together again in orbit around the far side of the Moon and preparing to fire *Casper*'s suspect engine. Would it, wouldn't it fire properly? Mission Control would not know until *Casper* re-established radio contact as it emerged over the lunar horizon. But the burn was good. Reported a relieved Mattingly: 'Morale around here just went up a couple hundred per cent.' Later, it was his turn to conduct a deep-space transearth EVA.

## Apollo 17: The geologist's mission

On all previous Apollo missions the lunar surface explorers had been astronauts trained in science. But on the final Apollo mission NASA, under considerable pressure from the scientific community, decided to include in the crew a trained scientist. He was geologist Harrison ('Jack') Schmitt, who was the first of a new breed of scientist-astronauts. Others of this breed participated in the Skylab missions and now fly routinely as payload specialists on shuttle and Spacelab flights.

Apollo 17 provided an appropriate fireworks finale to the Apollo program as it launched just after midnight on 7 December 1972. Schmitt and fellow-moonwalker Eugene Cernan flew the LM *Challenger* down to the surface, while Ronald Evans stayed in orbit in the CSM *America*.

*Challenger* set down at a site named Taurus-Littrow, close to the Taurus mountains and Littrow crater, on the eastern edge of the Sea of Serenity (Mare Serenitatis). Nicknamed Box canyon, it was a dramatic site, in a valley hemmed in by massifs at least 2000 meters (6500 feet) high. *Challenger* made a pinpoint landing, scarcely 90 meters (300 feet) off target, close to Camelot crater. This crater was named after the musical *Camelot*, a great favorite of the late President Kennedy.

The site was chosen for two main reasons. First, a landslide had brought down material from one of the high massifs, allowing the astronauts to sample rock from the heights without having to climb. Second, a close inspection of orbital photographs suggested the presence there of younger, fresher lava flows.

▶ The last Moon-landing mission this century, Apollo 17, lifts off spectacularly just after midnight on 7 December 1972. It is the only night-time launch of the Saturn V.

▶ 'Gardening' in the Taurus-Littrow valley during one of the three Apollo 17 EVAs is geologist Harrison Schmitt. He is using a lunar rake to collect rock chips of certain sizes.

## Losing a fender

When Schmitt emerged from the LM at the start of the first EVA, he looked around and declared the dramatic landscape around the landing site to be 'a geologist's paradise, if I've ever seen one'.

However, before the two moonwalkers set forth on what was to be an extraordinarily productive geological field trip, they had to unpack the lunar rover. Just afterwards an overenthusiastic Cernan smashed one of the fenders of the rover with a hammer. He carried out a makeshift repair with sticky tape, but as soon as they set out to explore, the fender fell off. Said Cernan in disgust: 'Oh, it pretty near makes me sick at losing that fender.'

The problem was not as trivial as it may seem. The purpose of the fender was to prevent the ever-present lunar dust spraying up from the wheels and covering the astronauts and their equipment. Eventually, with helpful suggestions from Mission Control, they made a passable repair by taping on plastic-coated map sheets.

When the serious business started, Schmitt was in his element, surveying all the geological nuances of his surroundings with a practised eye and providing expert commentary as he collected samples, chipped away at massive boulders and dug into the lunar soil. One spectacular find was a patch of bright orange soil at one of the small craters on the valley floor. It was the only real color astronauts had seen on the Moon. It looked so fresh; was it evidence of recent volcanic action?

During the mission Schmitt was often tempted to linger longer than the mission profile laid down. At one location near Van Serg crater where he dallied, Mission Contral tersely ordered him to get going 'immediately if not sooner'. 'We can't … we can't leave this,' Schmitt protested. 'This may be the youngest mantle over whatever was thrown out of the craters.' Science won out, and Schmitt stayed on.

Up in orbit lunar science was progressing in other directions. CSM

pilot Evans was surveying the lunar surface with the instruments of the SIM bay. The infrared scanners detected a number of unusually cold and unusually hot spots. He saw with his own eyes mysterious flashes of light, one near the Eastern Sea (Mare Orientale) and another near the prominent crater Eratosthenes. They were possible instances of volcanic gases venting from the lunar interior. Astronomers on Earth have witnessed similar happenings on the Moon, calling them transient lunar phenomena (TLP).

## The end of the beginning

Apollo 17 was the record-breaker. Three EVAs totalling more than 22 hours took Cernan, Schmitt and the rover more than 35 km (22 miles). They collected a record 115 kg (250 pounds) of rock, soil and core samples. Observed Schmitt before he left the 'geologist's paradise' at Taurus-Littrow: 'This valley has seen mankind complete his first evolutionary steps in the universe. I think no more significant contribution has Apollo made to history.'

During his last few minutes on the surface, Cernan spoke to young people of 78 nations who had been invited to Houston for the final Apollo mission. He held up 'a very significant rock, composed of many fragments of all sizes and shapes and colors'. He said that back on Earth the rock would be divided among their countries 'as a symbol that we can live in peace and harmony in the future'.

The world watched as the rover's TV camera saw *Challenger* shoot up spectacularly from the surface to mark the end of the first human exploration of man's nearest neighbor in space. The time was 5.55 pm EST (Eastern Standard Time) on 14 December 1972. In less than 10 minutes *Challenger* was back in lunar orbit and closing in on its mother ship *America*. Said Cernan as they approached *America*: 'God, you look pretty!'

After the dust-covered moonwalkers had transferred their treasure trove of samples and themselves into *America*, they despatched

◀ Another Apollo 17 photo-opportunity sees Harrison Schmitt pictured with the US flag and above it a gibbous Earth.

*Challenger* back whence it came to impact on the Moon. There it set the Moon ringing and the seismometers of the five ALSEP scientific stations jumping as it joined the other $520 million worth of equipment left behind by the 12 men from another world who had planted their footprints in Moondust.

Five days after leaving the Moon, Schmitt, Cernan and Evans were splashing down in the Pacific after notching up another record – the longest Moon mission, lasting 301 hours, 51 minutes and 59 seconds. Apollo was history.

Six successful Moon landings, one successful failure – all had been accomplished in the space of three and a half years. And it had only been four years since man first escaped from the clutches of the gravity that had bound him to Earth for the three million years of his existence.

Apollo had made it possible. Apollo had provided the giant leap that had opened up the space frontier to mankind. Apollo had set man's feet firmly on the stairway that must one day lead him to the stars.

▶ The Apollo 17 command module splashes down on 19 December 1972, bringing to an end the most remarkable chapter in the history of human exploration. Being winched up from the floating module here is CSM pilot Ronald Evans.

▼ The ascent stage of the lunar module *Challenger* moves slowly in to dock with the CSM *America*. Aboard are moonwalkers Harrison Schmitt and Eugene Cernan and 115 kg (250 pounds) of Moon rock, soil and core samples.

▶ When a very thin slice of Moon rock is examined under a microscope in special lighting conditions, its crystals show up in a kaleidoscope of colors. This is a sample of basalt rock brought back by the Apollo 12 astronauts.

# SIX

O N THE SURFACE and in orbit the Apollo astronauts launched a many pronged scientific assault on the Moon. The results of their endeavors are impressive and voluminous. Most valuable are the 385 kg (850 pounds) of rocks and soil the astronauts collected. Even today, only a fraction of the rock and soil samples have been thoroughly examined – modern techniques require only minute amounts for analysis. These samples not only reveal the nature of the Moon's surface, but also tell us its age. In addition they hold etched indelibly in their interior a record of the Sun's behavior for ages past.

Tens of thousands of reels of magnetic tape data resulted from the experiments the astronauts conducted on the surface and from orbit, using a bevy of sophisticated instruments, including magnetometers, seismometers, particle detectors, spectrometers and gravimeters. The five ALSEP stations provided a longer term study of the Moon's environment and in particular of its internal structure. They poured forth streams of data until September 1977, when lack of funds called a halt to the program.

Further invaluable insight into the lunar mystery was provided by the on-the-spot descriptions of the astronauts themselves, and by the 33,000 photographs they took. To the layman it is the photographs that provide the greatest legacy of the Apollo program. Even decades later, they remain stunning and hauntingly beautiful.

In general Apollo science showed there to be certain similarities between the Earth and the Moon, but also significant differences. Surprisingly, it detected traces of a magnetic field and even a whiff of 'atmosphere'. In some regions it found radioactive hotspots and curious concentrations of mass. Unsurprisingly, it found no traces of water or of organic life. None could exist on a world that is alternately baked and frozen every two weeks, constantly bombarded with meteorites and nakedly exposed to deadly ultraviolet radiation from the Sun and cosmic radiation from outer space.

# Reaping the Scientific Harvest

▼ At the Apollo 11 landing site on the Sea of Tranquillity, Edwin Aldrin uses a special tool to take a sample of the powdery lunar soil. The barren flat landscape is typical of that of the lunar seas.

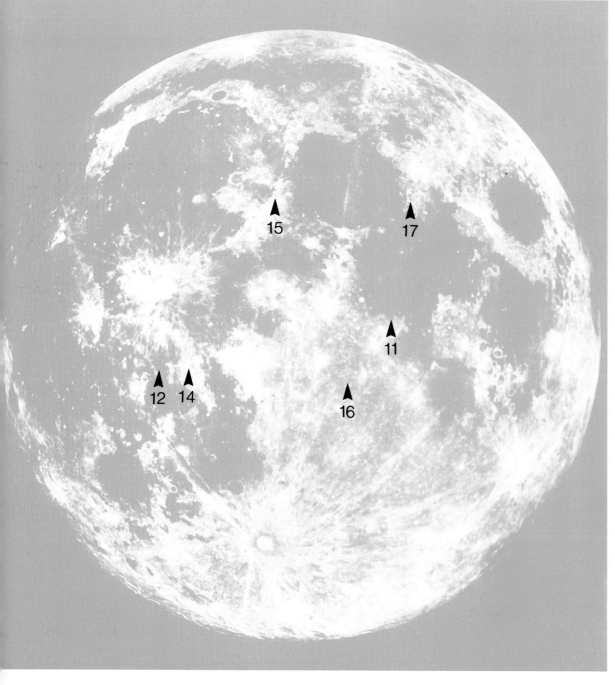

▼ The location of the Apollo landing sites on the lunar surface. The picture shows the full Moon as we see it from Earth. The Apollo astronauts often saw a different full Moon (see page 54).

## Reading the rocks

When the first Moon rocks were brought back to Earth, they, along with the astronauts who brought them, were placed in quarantine for three weeks. This procedure ceased after Apollo 14, by which time the lunar environment was pronounced sterile. First examination of the rocks was made at the Lunar Receiving Laboratory at the Johnson Space Center, Houston. From there, samples were later despatched to selected geologists throughout the world for detailed analysis.

The investigators tested the rocks with a variety of instruments to determine their chemical composition, magnetism, radioactivity and other physical properties. Among the most important analytical tools they used were the petrographic microscope and the electron microprobe.

The petrographic or geological microscope is used to examine thin sections of rock – slithers of rock ground and polished until they are thinner than a sheet of paper. In this form the rock becomes transparent. When examined in the microscope in polarized light, the crystalline structure of the rock shows up. The electron microprobe fires electrons at the rock sample and detects the different types of X-rays given out. These reveal which chemical elements are present in the sample.

Other tests determined how old the rocks are. They were dated using what are called radioactive clocks. Certain radioactive elements, such as uranium, decay or change into new elements as time goes by. By measuring the relative proportions of 'parent' and 'daughter' elements in a rock, the time that has elapsed since its formation can be estimated.

## The fire-formed rocks

On Earth there are three kinds of rocks. Igneous rocks are the 'fire-formed' rocks, formed when molten rock cooled on or near the surface. Sedimentary rocks are the accumulated layers of sediments deposited from ancient seas. Metamorphic rocks are formed when existing rocks are changed by heat and pressure within the Earth's crust.

On the Moon there are only igneous rocks, but different types are found in the maria and the highlands. The mare rocks are very similar to the kinds of igneous rock we know on Earth as basalt, formed when lava spewed out by volcanoes solidified on the surface. Lunar basalt is a dark rock containing tiny crystals, formed when the mare regions flooded with lava. Many of the basalts are riddled with holes, or vesicles, formed by gas bubbles in the cooling lava.

The minerals in lunar basalts are similar to those in terrestrial ones and include pyroxene, olivine, ilmenite and feldspar. Compared with

◀ Made up of cemented rock fragments, this is a typical lunar breccia. Examples are found all over the Moon, on the great lava plains and in the highlands.

▼ This volcanic rock came from the Apollo 15 site near Hadley rille. Riddled with holes, it is nicknamed 'Vuggy' by geologists (a 'vug' is a cavity).

▼ At the Lunar Receiving Laboratory at Houston, test director Daniel Anderson examines a chunk of Moon rock brought back from Fra Mauro by the Apollo 14 astronauts.

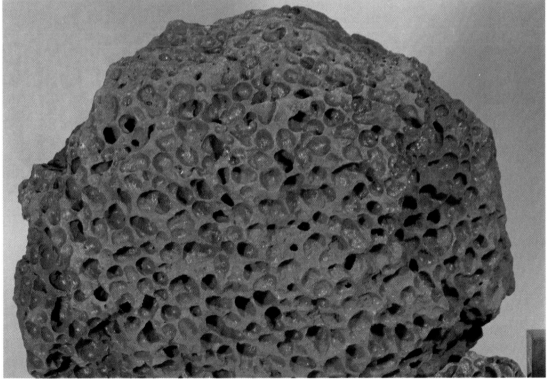

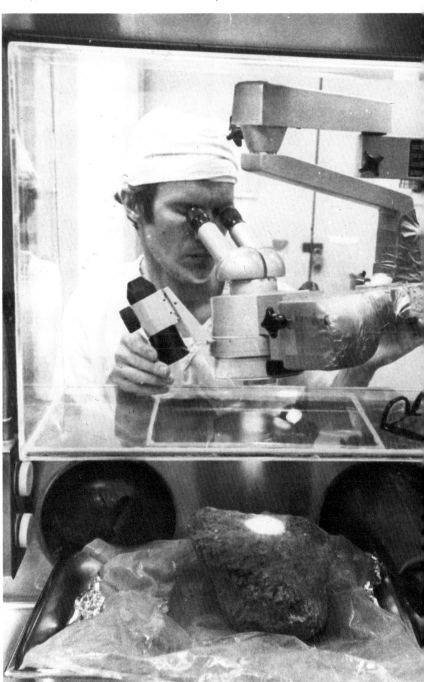

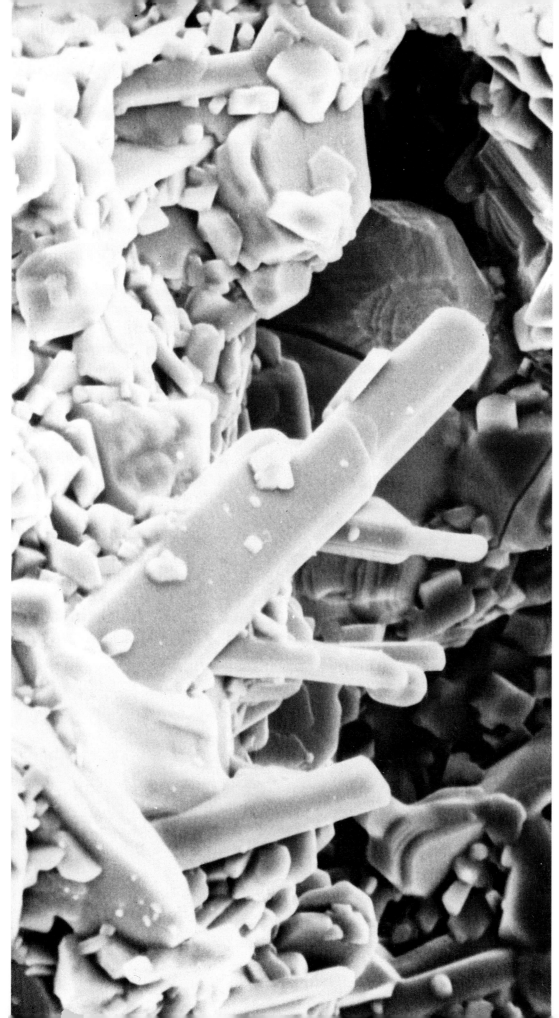

◀ A scanning electron microscope took this photograph of a nest of crystals in a small cavity in a sample of breccia brought back from Fra Mauro (Apollo 14). The long crystals are pyroxene (magnesium iron silicate) and the short ones plagioclase feldspar. Small crystals of ilmenite are also present. All the minerals resemble minerals found on Earth.

Earth basalt, however, the lunar basalt contains more titanium and iron. A new titanium mineral, which has no equivalent on Earth, was found in several lunar basalts. It has been named armalcolite, after the first letters of the names of the Apollo 11 astronauts.

The igneous rocks of the highlands are lighter in color and weight than the mare basalts. They are also quite different in composition. They contain much more calcium and aluminum and a high proportion of feldspar, and are similar to the terrestrial rocks called gabbro. Some, however, are made up almost entirely of feldspar and resemble a type of rock called anorthosite, which is extremely rare on Earth.

The age of the lunar basalts from the maria ranges from about 3.2 billion years for an Apollo 12 rock to more than 3.8 billion years for an Apollo 17 sample. This age range covers the period when lava welled up from the Moon's interior to create the maria. The highland rocks are older than the mare basalts, dating from 4 to 4.2 billion years. The highlands are what remains of the Moon's original crust.

### The meteorite onslaught

Throughout its history, the Moon has been bombarded with meteorites, particles of matter ranging in size from grains of sand to huge boulders. The evidence of this bombardment is visible everywhere in the craters large and small that pockmark the lunar surface. In the past large meteorites have slammed into the lunar rocks and shattered them to pieces. The force of the impacts caused some of the rock to melt, and this cemented together the shattered pieces to form a new kind of rock. It is called breccia after a similar rock containing rock chips found on Earth.

Breccias are found all over the Moon, particularly in the highlands. At two of the highland landing sites, Apollo 14 and 16, breccia rock covers the landscape in thick blankets. These are thought to have been formed following the catastrophic impacts of the massive meteorites or asteroids that created the vast lava basins we know as the Sea of Showers (Mare Imbrium) and the Eastern Sea (Mare Orientale).

### Lunar gardening

The constant bombardment of the Moon by meteorites gradually pulverizes the surface into a kind of loose, dusty 'soil', which scientists call regolith. It is the major process of erosion that reshapes the lunar surface.

The Apollo astronauts found dusty soil everywhere. In fact it was a decided nuisance, clinging to clothing, tools, cameras and anything it came into contact with. When the dust-covered sample bags from Apollo 11 were being opened, several technicians at the Lunar

Receiving Laboratory accidentally became covered in the sticky dust and had to join the astronauts in quarantine.

The soil is made up of rock fragments, bits of crystals and a high proportion of glass. The glass, clear or colored green, orange and red, is present mainly as little spheres. These were formed when meteorites hit and melted the surface material and caused it to be ejected. As the ejected matter traveled, it formed naturally into little spheres. Large amounts of ejected glasses are thought to be responsible for the prominent rays that radiate out from many of the large lunar craters, such as Archimedes and Tycho. On the ground the glass spheres often make the soil slippery to walk on, contributing to many a slip by the Apollo astronauts.

To a certain extent the impacts of fresh meteorite material rework the surface soil, and the process has been called gardening. But it is a slow process. The Apollo astronauts bored into the soil at the various landing sites to take core samples. When these were examined, they were found in general to contain many distinct layers of material and showed little evidence of gardening.

**The solar connection**
The Moon is bombarded not only by tangible chunks of meteorite material, but also by streams of invisible particles streaming out from the Sun and from outer space. The particles streaming out from the Sun form what is called the solar wind. Its main constituents are electrically charged atoms of hydrogen and helium. This is to be expected because they are the main elements that make up the Sun. When these atoms strike the Moon, they are absorbed as gas by the surface layers, or they react chemically with other elements in the rocks and soil.

The hydrogen and helium gases gradually filter out of the surface and appear to be mainly responsible for the thin lunar atmosphere, which the Apollo instruments unexpectedly detected. Neon and argon were other gases detected in the atmosphere. The neon almost certainly comes from the solar wind, while the argon probably comes from inside the Moon itself, resulting from the decay of radioactive potassium in the rocks.

The solar wind particles make tiny but detectable tracks in the rocks. They normally are not very energetic and do not penetrate very far in − less than one-thousandth of a millimeter. However, at times of solar flares − massive eruptions on the Sun − the solar wind 'blows gale force', and its particles can penetrate as deep as 6 cm (nearly 2½ inches). They act as miniature atom smashers and convert some atoms in the rocks into different atoms.

Even more penetrating are the charged atoms that bombard the Moon from outer space. These so-called cosmic rays have very high

▼ In the foreground of this photograph of the Apollo 11 landing site is a seismometer, designed to record moonquakes. Study of these 'quakes helps scientists determine what the Moon is like inside.

▶ Here at Fra Mauro the Apollo 14 astronauts have set up the instrument package known as ALSEP to form an automatic scientific station. The instruments are linked to a central transmitting station (center), which relays instrument readings to scientists on Earth. The station receives electricity from a nuclear power unit known as RTG (radioisotope thermoelectric generator).

energy indeed and can penetrate rocks to a depth of up to 2 meters (6.5 feet). Again, they leave tracks and bring about nuclear transformations.

Analysis of the type of particle track, depth of penetration and number of changed atoms in Moon rocks provides a way of estimating how long the rocks have been buried or exposed and how they have moved through the lunar soil. More importantly, they provide an insight into the past history of the Sun. It appears from Apollo data that the solar wind has been 'blowing' steadily for at least a billion years. There are no indications in the data that the Sun's energy output is increasing or decreasing. This is a comforting thought because only a fractional change in solar energy output either way could spell the end of life on Earth as we know it.

### Ringing like a bell

The Earth, we believe, is made up of several layers of rocks. The thin outer crust overlays a thick layer of heavier rock called the mantle. At the center is a solid inner core, around which is an outer liquid core, both made up, we think, of iron and nickel. How do we know this? From measurements taken by sensitive seismometers of the way shock waves triggered off by earthquakes travel through the Earth.

It was one of the major aims of all the Apollo missions except the last to set up seismic stations on the Moon to investigate 'moonquakes', if there were any. From the seismic data, the internal structure of the Moon could then be determined.

The seismometer the Apollo 11 astronauts set up worked for only three weeks. But the others formed part of the ALSEP scientific stations and worked for several years. Since nothing was known about the lunar interior beforehand, a means was needed for calibrating the instruments so that recorded events could be correctly located and interpreted.

For calibration, artificial moonquakes were produced by deliberately crashing on to the Moon parts of Apollo hardware. The most effective impacts were made by the 14-tonne third stage (the SIVB) of the Saturn V launch rocket that injected the Apollo spacecraft into translunar trajectory and then accompanied it to the Moon. Other impacts were made using the 2½-tonne lunar module after it had ferried the two moonwalkers back into orbit.

The first artificial moonquake, made by the Apollo 12 SIVB on the Ocean of Storms, produced a total surprise. The seismometer registered the impact with a sharp vibration. But instead of dying away, the vibration continued strongly for some time, fading away only after about two hours. 'The Moon', said one scientist, 'rang like a bell.' On Earth a similar seismic signal would have died away in minutes.

From such results, reinforced by seismic readings from the other ALSEP stations, scientists concluded that the upper layer of the Moon's crust must be formed of cracked and broken rock. This would enable the shock waves made by such impacts to echo back and forth and produce the observed 'ringing'.

Beneath the broken-rock layer come other layers of crust, apparently formed of different types of rocks. Down to about 25 km (15 miles) the rock seems to be basalt. Then comes a gabbro-type rock down to about 65 km (40 miles). Below this level is the lunar mantle, probably of heavier rock, which continues down to about 800 km (500 miles). Many moonquakes originate at this level or below, and it is possible that it marks the beginning of a partly molten transition layer between the solid mantle and a molten core. But whether or not the core is metallic like the Earth's is unknown.

### Daughter, wife or sister?

What light did the Apollo findings shed on the origin of the Moon? Traditionally there are three main theories about its origin. The fission or escape theory sees the Moon as the Earth's daughter. The Earth was once much larger, but early in its history it split into two, the smaller of the pieces becoming the Moon. The capture theory sees the Moon as the Earth's wife. It suggests that the Moon formed as a separate body elsewhere in the solar system and was eventually flung by gravitational force into an orbit that took it close enough to the Earth to be captured by its gravity. The third, double-planet theory sees the Moon as the Earth's sister. It was formed where it is now at the same time as the Earth.

The Apollo science results did not come down firmly in favor of any theory. The chemical differences between lunar and terrestrial rocks argue against the Earth and Moon ever having been the same body or been formed in situ from similar primeval material. This would seem to point to a capture theory. But the mechanism by which the Moon could have been formed somewhere else and ended up where it is now cannot be fathomed. And on balance, astronomers put their bets on the Earth-Moon system being a double planet. Further exploration of the Moon next century could prove them right — or wrong.

▲ The Apollo 15 CSM *Endeavour* in lunar orbit, showing its open scientific instrument bay (SIM). The results obtained from SIM scans make a major contribution to lunar science, leading to the discovery of mascons and radioactive hotspots.

◄ At the Johnson Space Center, Houston, on 30 September 1977, seismometer readings relayed back from the ALSEP stations are taken for the last time, signaling the end of Apollo lunar science.

◀ Skylab 3 astronaut Owen Garriott working near the ATM during the first of three EVAs during the mission. He has just loaded new film canisters into the ATM's telescope-cameras. His EVA lasts a record 6½ hours.

▼ One of the 183,000 images of our nearest star, the Sun, taken with Skylab's solar instruments. It shows the most spectacular prominence ever witnessed, a fountain of fiery gas looping high above the Sun's surface.

69

# SEVEN

# Spin-offs Skylab and ASTP

USING SURPLUS APOLLO HARDWARE, NASA launched in 1973 the biggest spacecraft there had ever been. It measured 28 meters (90 feet) long and weighed the best part of 75 tonnes. It was as spacious as a two-bedroomed house. This colossus of a spacecraft was an experimental space station called Skylab. Although it nearly met its end during launch, it went on to provide a home for three teams of astronauts for record-breaking periods of 28, 56 and 84 days.

In its own way Skylab represented as momentous a leap forward in space exploration as the Apollo Moon missions. The Skylab astronauts conducted more than 50 major experiments into the biological, medical, physical, engineering and astronomical sciences. They made an in-depth study of the Sun, acquiring more data over a nine-month period than all the solar scientists on Earth could do in a century.

More important for the long-term future of humankind in space, the Skylab astronauts proved without doubt that, with proper diet and exercise, human beings could live and work for long periods in the weightlessness of space without suffering permanent harm. They also demonstrated how invaluable is the human touch when things start to go wrong in space. Without the astronauts' DIY talents the project would have been doomed from the start. Of less importance scientifically, but of great significance politically, was the final Apollo-derived mission, the ASTP (Apollo-Soyuz Test Project), which took place in July 1975. The ASTP was the first international manned space flight, which saw arch rivals America and Russia come together in a spirit of what would in the Gorbachev era come to be known as glasnost.

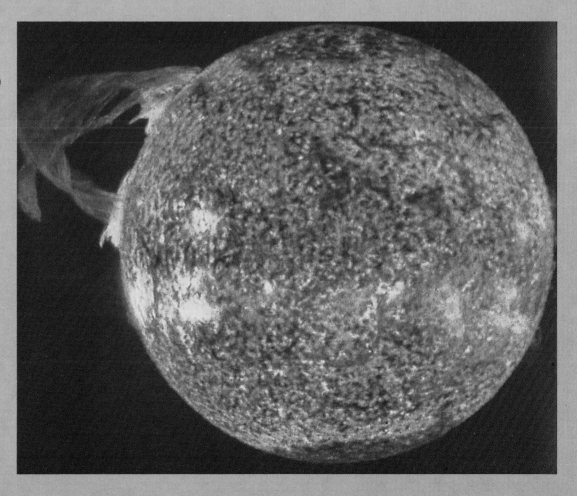

▶ A Saturn IB rocket launches each of the manned Skylab missions. On the launch pad designed for the much taller Saturn V, it has to blast off from a high tower. The picture shows the launch of Skylab 4 on 16 November 1973. The astronauts would not return to Earth for nearly three months.

## Birth of a space station

The presidential and public euphoria that accompanied the first successful Moon landing was short-lived. People began to ask what were the practical benefits of exploring the Moon. It was not enough to go to the Moon because it's there, was it cost effective? Arguments that it opened up new horizons in the study of the solar system and the universe at large fell on deaf ears. The result was that the last three Moon-landing missions originally projected, Apollo 18, 19 and 20, were axed.

This dealt a body blow to NASA but meant that they now had at their disposal redundant Apollo hardware. They were not slow to take advantage of the situation.

As early as 1965 plans had been made for an Earth-orbiting station as part of what came to be called the Apollo Applications Program (AAP). But budget cuts and switched resources for command-module modifications following the Apollo 1 fire caused NASA to re-think the whole Earth-station idea. When a Saturn V launch vehicle became available after the cancellation of the later Moon-landing missions, plans were finalized for an Earth-orbiting space station, which in 1970 was given the name Skylab.

## The Skylab cluster

The space station was built around a redundant SIVB rocket stage. The stage itself formed the main part of Skylab, the orbital workshop (OWS), which served as living quarters for the crew and as a laboratory and workshop for carrying out experiments. At the forward end of the OWS, the airlock module (AM) led into the multiple docking adapter (MDA), which had two docking ports. The three-man crews were ferried up to Skylab in modified Apollo CSMs, which docked at the aft port of the MDA.

The Apollo telescope mount (ATM) was another module mounted on the MDA. It housed a package of telescopes and sensors for studying the Sun. It also carried a windmill-like set of panels, which held solar cells to generate electricity for the station. As designed, the OWS carried two other solar panels.

When the CSM was docked at the MDA, the whole Skylab cluster measured no less than 36 meters (119 feet) long. Up in orbit some 435 km (270 miles) high, it reflected sunlight brilliantly. Under clear skies it was readily visible from many parts of the world, including all of the United States except Alaska, South America, China, Africa, Australia and most of Asia. It was like a slowly moving and steadily shining 'shooting star', as bright as the brightest stars in the sky. Other debris could be seen ahead of and behind Skylab, the brightest being the Saturn II second-stage rocket that accompanied the space station into orbit.

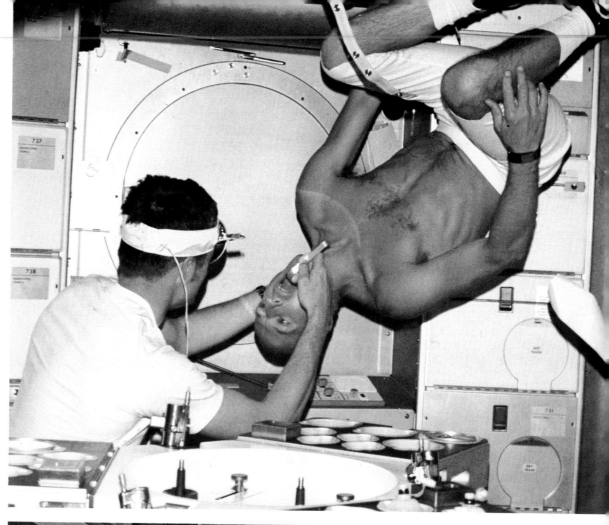

## The Skylab parasol

The launch plan called for Skylab to be launched by a Saturn V rocket one day, and then the first crew would follow it the day after. On 14 May 1973 the Saturn V blasted off the pad in what looked like a perfect launch. But telemetry recorded that a meteoroid shield designed to protect the space station in orbit had deployed prematurely only a minute into the flight. As it tore away, it carried with it one of the OWS solar panels and for good measure jammed the other. When Skylab reached orbit, its temperature began to soar as the merciless heat of the Sun penetrated into the station through the damaged area.

The projected launch next day of the first Skylab crew of Charles Conrad, Joseph Kerwin and Paul Weitz was postponed until 25 May, by which time NASA had worked out, it hoped, a means of fixing the ailing space station. And so it proved.

In two vital spacewalks the crew erected a sunshade, or parasol, over the damaged outer skin and freed the remaining solar panel on the OWS. Within hours the temperature inside the space station began to fall to a comfortable level, and it began to receive the extra power it needed to support the projected long-term habitation and the ambitious experimental workload.

There were many more glitches as the Skylab program proceeded apace, but the astronauts, in cahoots with teams of engineers on the ground, were always able to cope. The first Skylab crew returned after 28 days in orbit, none the worse for the longest duration space flight so far. On 28 July the next crew of Alan Bean, Owen Garriott and Jack Lousma rendezvoused with the station and remained there for 59 days. On the final mission Gerald Carr, Edward Gibson and William Pogue headed up into orbit on 16 November, not returning until the following February after traveling 55 million km (34 million miles) in 84 days.

## Skylab science

Skylab housed the biggest collection of scientific instruments ever flown into orbit. The astronauts carried out investigations into four main areas – medical, Earth-resources, solar and technological.

The medical experiments centered on studying man's ability to work and live for prolonged periods under zero-gravity conditions. The astronauts used themselves as guinea pigs, taking blood samples, measuring fluid intake and excretion, monitoring heart beat and blood circulation at rest and after exercise, for example on the Skylab bicycle ergonometer. Regular workouts on the ergonometer provided the astronauts with the main means of exercise during their long missions.

And it kept them surprisingly fit. The final Skylab crew found

▲ Going to the dentist on Earth was never like this! Skylab 1 astronaut Charles Conrad finds it comfortable to hang upside-down to have his teeth examined by doctor-in-residence Joseph Kerwin. During their long stints in orbit the Skylab astronauts check one another over regularly to see how their bodies cope with the problem of prolonged weightlessness.

◀ In zero-gravity balancing a man on the tip of your finger is as easy as – standing on your head! Here, in the spacious upper compartment of the orbital workshop during the final Skylab mission, Edward Gibson demonstrates how to do it, with the assistance of bearded Gerald Carr.

little difficulty in adapting to normal gravity, even after being weightless for 12 weeks.

In their Earth-resources experiments the Skylab astronauts used a set of six instruments and cameras (the EREP – Earth Resources Experiment Package) to observe the Earth, making a valuable contribution to the emerging art of remote sensing. The images they acquired provided valuable resource material for use in many fields, including agriculture and forestry, geology and geography, meteorology and oceanography.

In materials science experiments the astronauts studied crystal growth and manufactured new alloys in the unique zero-gravity conditions. In the biological sciences they carried out a range of experiments suggested by high-school students, which ranged from incubating bacteria to studying how well spiders spun their webs in weightlessness.

But the most astonishing results came from the solar observations made by the astronauts with the eight instruments mounted in the ATM. They monitored and directed the instruments from a control console in the MDA. The instruments probed the Sun at many different wavelengths. They spied the most spectacular prominences – fountains of fiery gas that arced hundreds of thousands of kilometers above the surface. Another astronomical bonus was provided on the final Skylab mission by the first (and maybe the last) visit to Earthly skies of Comet Kohoutek. Skylab's observations – the first of a comet from space – helped shed more light on the nature and origin of these mysterious visitors from the distant depths of the solar system.

### Handshake in orbit

Americans did not return to orbit until July 1975, when they joined their Russian counterparts in a joint flight that demonstrated that cooperation between the great space powers was a practical proposition. The mission was the Apollo-Soyuz Test Project. For the joint flight to be possible, both the Apollo and Soyuz spacecraft had to be modified. In particular Apollo flew into orbit with a custom-built docking module attached, which was compatible with the Soyuz docking mechanism.

On 15 July Soyuz took off from the Baikonur Cosmodrome in Central Russia. On board were veteran cosmonaut Alexei Leonov, who had pioneered spacewalking 10 years before, and Valery Kubasov. Apollo followed hours later from the Kennedy Space Center, half a world away. Thomas Stafford commanded the crew, who also included Donald Slayton, one of the 'Original Seven' Mercury astronauts, and Vance Brand.

Two days later over Europe the two craft docked together. The

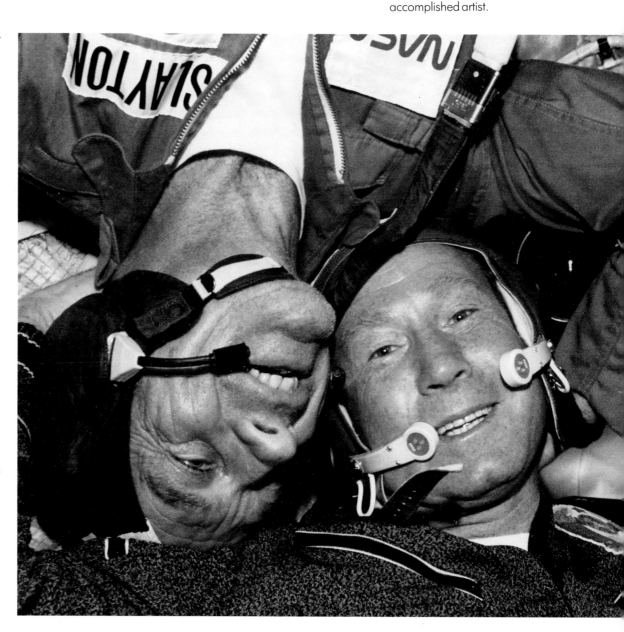

hatches were opened and the two crews shook hands to cement bonds of friendship and respect between guys with the 'Right Stuff' from the two great spacefaring nations.

On 24 July, the blackened Apollo command module returned to Earth to bring the Apollo series of manned missions to a close. For the United States it was the end of the expendable era of manned spaceflight. The next time its astronauts sped into orbit, it would be in a revolutionary new vehicle, the re-usable space shuttle. But that would not be for another six years.

### The final chapter

The ASTP mission, which *Time* described as a 'celestial handclasp between old adversaries', was not quite the end of the Apollo story. Remaining in orbit was space station Skylab, mothballed by the final Skylab team when they left it in February 1974. Because of its size, NASA knew that Skylab would gradually drift closer to Earth as it was slowed down by the tenuous outer atmosphere. But before it came too close, the planned space shuttle should be ready and able to boost Skylab into a higher orbit, perhaps to be used again.

However, it was not to be. Violent sunspot activity on the Sun in 1977 and 1978 caused thickening of the outer atmosphere, which greatly increased drag on Skylab. By 1979 the space station had fallen to a perilously low orbit. The launch of the space shuttle was still years away. Nothing could be done to prevent Skylab finally succumbing to gravity and plunging back to Earth.

The prospect of 75 tonnes of Skylab hardware raining down on the Earth was potentially a grim one. Although it would break up during re-entry through the atmosphere, chunks of up to 2 tonnes could survive, traveling at up to 500 km/h (300 mph). If these chunks fell in an urban area, property could be damaged and people could be killed.

In the event, due perhaps more to luck than judgement, Skylab began breaking up over the Indian Ocean. But it left a long 'footprint'. Its final death throes did not occur until it was over Western Australia. The inhabitants of Perth were treated to a spectacular fireworks display as flaming debris streaked overhead.

The date was 11 July. The re-entry fireworks of Skylab, son of Apollo, had come just five days before the 10th anniversary of Apollo 11's triumphant ascent into the heavens, destination Moon.

This is the breathtakingly beautiful landscape where man last set foot on the Moon, the valley of Taurus-Littrow. Geologist Harrison Schmitt is seen working near the lunar rover. To the layman such photographs provide one of the greatest legacies of Apollo.

# 'We Shall Return in Peace and Hope for all Mankind'

# EPILOG

GALILEO IT WAS who began the scientific study of the Moon when he trained his newly made telescope on it in 1609. He it was who discovered that our nearest neighbor in space was not the goddess or the perfect sphere beloved of philosophers, but an imperfect, blemished alternative world with its own unique geography of vast arid seas and rugged mountain ranges pock-marked with craters. Three hundred and sixty years later we knew this for certain when Neil Armstrong became the first of 12 Apollo astronauts to plant their footprints in the lunar soil.

The technological tour de force that was Apollo opened up a new era in man's history. *The Washington Post* observed after Armstrong's first small step: 'The creature who had once stood blinking at the door of his paleolithic cave has come a long way. No longer is he tied … to the world where he was born. The heavens lie open. The time nears when he will roam his solar system. Man is on the brink of mastering the universe.'

But was it worth it? Did Apollo justify the $25 billion lavished on it through the last Moon landing? Even today the arguments for and against still rage. On the one hand, Apollo reaped a rich scientific harvest; it brought about quantum leaps in technology from which we still benefit; it gave employment to upwards of half a million people; it provided a morale boost to the nation and inspiration to all peoples of the world.

On the other hand, could not the money have been spent on more down-to-Earth projects to benefit humankind more directly, to help eradicate the root causes of wars, poverty and suffering? History, however, indicates otherwise. The politicians who hold the purse strings are seldom able for a host of reasons to switch resources in this way. And statistically, the sum of $25 billion must be seen in perspective. It represented in round figures an expenditure of less than $20 per person per year for the decade of the 1960s. Over the same period Americans spent an average of about $180 each per year on cigarettes, beer and liquor.

A more intangible spin-off from Apollo was that it gave rise to the concept of spaceship Earth, to the realization that our planet, which teems with life in infinite variety and complexity, is unique, certainly in the solar system and maybe in the universe. James Lovell, commander of the ill-fated Apollo 13 mission, had more reason than most to appreciate the uniqueness of our home planet. He called it 'a grand oasis in the vastness of space'. That is what Earth is, a beautiful oasis of life, color and warmth in the limitless dead, dark and cold desert of space. We abuse and pollute this oasis at our peril.

There is nowhere else for us to go – at least, not yet. But thanks to Apollo we know that we need not be shackled to the Earth for ever. There is a whole universe out there.

Apollo 17 commander Eugene Cernan took the last step on the Moon on 14 December 1972. As he climbed back into the lunar module he was moved to make a promise: 'We leave as we came and, God willing, we shall return with peace and hope for all mankind.'

Early next century man will return to the Moon, this time for keeps. Astronaut-scientists and engineers will set up a permanent base to support astronomical and mining activities, and to act as a spaceport for interplanetary craft.

# Apollo Log

**1961**

*5 May:* On Mercury 3, the first manned mission in Project Mercury, Alan P. Shepard makes a 15-minute suborbital flight in Mercury capsule *Freedom 7*.

*25 May:* President John F. Kennedy exhorts the American nation to spare no effort to reach the goal of landing astronauts on the Moon, within the decade.

*21 July:* On Mercury 4 mission, Virgil I. Grissom makes a 15-minute suborbital flight in capsule *Liberty Bell 7*.

**1962**

*20 February:* On Mercury 6 mission, John H. Glenn makes the first American orbital flight in *Friendship 7*; 3 orbits.

*24 May:* On Mercury 7 mission, M. Scott Carpenter in *Aurora 7* becomes the second American into orbit; 3 orbits.

*11 July:* NASA selects lunar orbit rendezvous (LOR) as the technique for achieving manned a lunar landing.

*3 October:* On Mercury 8 mission, Walter M. Schirra in *Sigma 7* makes a 6-orbit flight.

**1963**

*15 May:* On Mercury 9, the final mission in Project Mercury, L. Gordon Cooper makes a 22-orbit flight in *Faith 7*.

**1964**

*28 July:* Ranger 7 launched; impacts on the Sea of Clouds (Mare Nubium) after sending back the first close-up photographs (over 4000) of the lunar surface.

*27 October:* Major-General Samuel C. Phillips, USAF, is appointed Director of the Apollo program.

**1965**

*17 February:* Ranger 8 launched to the Sea of Tranquillity (Mare Tranquillitatis); returns over 7000 photographs.

*21 March:* Ranger 9 launched to crater Alphonsus; returns nearly 6000 photographs.

*23 March:* Gemini 3, first mission in the two-man Gemini program, lifts off; crew Virgil I. Grissom, John W. Young; 3 orbits; capsule is the only one codenamed, *Molly Brown*.

*14 April:* Main structure of the Vehicle Assembly Building (VAB) is completed at the Kennedy Space Center.

*3 June:* Gemini 4 launched; crew James A. McDivitt, Edward H. White; White makes first American spacewalk; 62 orbits.

*21 August:* Gemini 5 launched; crew Charles Conrad, L. Gordon Cooper; 120 orbits.

*4 December:* Gemini 7 launched; crew Frank Borman, James A. Lovell; performs first in-orbit rendezvous with Gemini 6; 206 orbits.

*15 December:* Gemini 6 launched; crew Thomas P. Stafford, Walter M. Schirra; rendezvous with Gemini 7; 16 orbits.

**1966**

*26 February:* Launch of Apollo-Saturn 201 (AS-201); first flight (unmanned) of the Saturn IB/SIVB combination, with dummy CM (command module); first CM recovery; first use of Mission Control Center at Houston for Apollo control.

*16 March:* Gemini 8 launched; crew Neil A. Armstrong, David R. Scott; makes first docking in space, with Agena target vehicle; 6 orbits.

*30 May:* Surveyor 1 launched; makes the first true soft-landing on the Moon near crater Flamsteed; returns over 11,000 photographs.

*3 June:* Gemini 9 launched; crew Eugene A. Cernan, Thomas P. Stafford; 44 orbits.

*5 July:* Launch of AS-203 (unmanned) with redesigned SIB; first orbital flight of SIVB.

*18 July:* Gemini 10 launched; crew John W. Young, Michael Collins; 43 orbits.

*10 August:* Lunar Orbiter 1 launched to survey the Moon's surface from orbit; sends back over 300 photographs.

*25 August:* Launch of AS-202 (unmanned), demonstrating launch escape system, separation of CM from SM (service module), operation of on-board systems; first Pacific recovery of CM.

*12 September:* Launch of Gemini 11; crew Charles Conrad, Richard F. Gordon; 44 orbits.

*20 September:* Surveyor 2 launched; mission fails.

*6 November:* Lunar Orbiter 2 launched; photographs 13 Apollo primary landing sites; sends back over 400 photographs.

*11 November:* Launch of Gemini 12, last in the series; crew James A. Lovell, Edwin E. Aldrin; 59 orbits.

**1967**

*27 January:* Astronauts Virgil I. Grissom, Edward H. White and Roger B. Chaffee are killed in a flash fire while training for the first manned flight, AS-204 or Apollo 1, scheduled for 21 February 1967.

*5 February:* Lunar Orbiter 3 launched; sends back over 300 photographs.

*17 April:* Surveyor 3C launched to Ocean of Storms (Oceanus Procellarum); sends back over 6000 photographs; conducts soil physics experiments.

*4 May:* Lunar Orbiter 4 launched; returned over 300 pictures.

*14 July:* Surveyor 4 launched; mission fails.